Spark

Igniting the Flame of Wisdom

Venerable Ācariya Thoon
Khippapanyo

Spark

Igniting the Flame of Wisdom

Original Thai text written by
Venerable Ācariya Thoon Khippapanyo
(Phra Banyāpisantaera)
Wat Pa Ban Kho
Udon Thani, Thailand

English translation by
Neecha Thian-Ngern
San Francisco, CA

Cover design by
Veerakeat Tongpaiboon

ISBN: 978-1-935207-00-9
Retail Price: $11.95

Translator's Note

The original Thai version of this text is entitled "The History of Buddha." For the English translation the title, "Spark: Igniting the Flame of Wisdom" was chosen because of the significance of the various sparks that ignited and motivated Buddha's wisdom development and ultimately, his holy enlightenment. From the visit to Kapilavastu, to the golden tray, to the very identification of *sammādiṭṭhi* as the starting point of all wisdom development, these crucial sparks are highlighted and emphasized in this text. The metaphor of the flame is also quite telling as wisdom, when cultivated, provides warmth and bright light for a practitioner. Once a flame is lit, it continues to burn just as a practitioner's wisdom will continue to grow with the right fuel in the form of *sammādiṭṭhi* and *paññā*.

This English translation is quite literal, and every effort has been made to maintain the integrity of the original work by Venerable Ācariya Thoon Khippapanyo. The greatest discrepancy between the Thai and English languages is the prevalence of the English personal pronoun and the Thai's lack thereof. Many Pali terms have multiple definitions such as *paññā* which denotes wisdom, insight, knowledge, and thought. As such, some Pali terms were used consistently throughout this text while others were translated in order to better capture the essence of the definition in each individual situation. I apologize in advance for any mistranslations or misinterpretations. May all of the efforts of those involved in this translation bear fruit as this book serves as a spark that ignites the flame of wisdom in the dhamma practice of the reader.

Preface

The book you are about to read, "Spark: Igniting the Flame of Wisdom," concerns the history of Buddha. This topic has been written about in many countries. In various parts, some are alike, while some are not. Thus, I have written this from yet another angle in order for you all to understand. Although there may be some discrepancies, the main takeaway is the enlightenment of Buddha and the parallel for internalized reflection that he used. The texts in existence lack clarity as to which resources Buddha employed to teach himself. From this text you all will be able to understand the importance of the golden tray. Buddha utilized the golden tray as a parallel to reflect on his own mind. He used discernment to generate wisdom, which is deemed *ñāṇatassana*, righteous perception, and experiences according to the truths of the world. By producing contentment and strong attachment to *kāmaguṇa* (worldly pleasures). insatiable desires are both the root and factors of birth. This is the very cause of endless rebirth for humans in the Three Realms. Buddha used the *paññāñāṇa* (insight-wisd om) that arose to cut off the force of desire from his conscious. In that very moment Buddha generated *sammādiṭṭhi*, the correct perception of the truth. Thus, he proclaimed to himself that the method used for enlightenment as a Buddha was individually known with *sati* (mindfulness), *sammādhi*, (concentration), and *paññā* (discernment). No one was his master. This indicates that *sammādiṭṭhi* (the correct perception of the truth) and *sammāsaṅkappa* (the right motive) are the starting point for dhamma practice.

I hope that you all read this book with mindfulness and discernment, using reason for contemplation. You will understand the history of Buddha, along with the method and resources used to practice dhamma that are aligned with the path to enlightenment.

Table of Contents

Translator's Note	i
Preface	iii
The History of Buddha	1
Life as a Child and Young Adult	5
Visit to Kapilavastu	11
Encountering the Four Divine Messengers	18
Ordination as an Ascetic	23
Finding the Path to Enlightenment on His Own	31
Discernment Used to Teach Oneself to Acquire Expansive Knowledge	35
Contemplating the Physical Aggregates	38
The Cause of Birth within the Three Realms	42
Unavoidable Suffering	49

The Emergence of Buddha's Wisdom 54
Abhiññā 62
Āsavakkhayañāṇa Occurs 67
Discernment of Noble Persons is Difficult 74
The Buddha's Meditation 78
Sammādiṭṭhi is the Foundation of Practice 81
Research the History of Arriyapuggala 88
Paññāvimutti and Cetovimutti 96
Discernment to Contemplate the Three Common Characteristics 106
Resources for Dhamma Practice 112
Interpret Buddha's Teachings Well 117
Selecting the Proper Leader 126
Abhidhamma 128
Conclusion 132
About the Author 140
About the Translator 142

The History of Buddha

The history of Buddha is read by Buddhists throughout the world. The existence of similarities and differences in writing is attributed the discrepancies in perception. Younger generations read and understand according to those very perceptions. In some countries there is partially sufficient evidence, while in other countries there is not.

In the year 1962, I had the opportunity to cross the border to Laos and stayed at the Dong Na Chok Temple. I like to study and I had come across a bookshelf containing an old copy of the *Tipiṭaka* (Pali Canon) written on dried palm leaves. It was written in the Laotian language and there were many copies of the book carefully wrapped in cloth. Once I unwrapped the covering, it was obvious the book was Buddha's history. I was interested to investigate whether or not the Laotian and Thai versions would differ. There were many elements that diverged, while others were similar. This text will not delve into some of those differences.

In 2004, I visited Luang Phra Bang for the purpose of searching for old versions of Buddha's history, but I could not find any. I asked many elder monks where these older copies were stored and they replied that the books were destroyed during the change in government. The copies we have left in the present are Thai versions written in the Laotian language.

After reading the Laotian version of Buddha's history at that time, I remembered clearly what I had read because of its reason and credibility. I will present selections which I believe are important for the reader to acknowledge. I would like to highlight the story of Prince Siddhāttha's ordination as an ascetic. This account differs slightly from the Thai version. I believe those of you who are knowledgeable will rationally acknowledge this, as Buddhism in each country has portrayed this differently. Whichever version is the most credible in terms of reason should be considered.

When Buddha was alive, **he stated that in the distant future, there will be dissent among Buddhist views. The written foundations of Buddha's teachings will both deviate and be incorrect. Therefore, Buddhists in that era will misunderstand Buddha's teaching a great deal. Those who practice in that age will be confused. Initiation of dhamma practice will not be based on the same foundations that Buddha delineated.** As illustrated in the *Kālāmasutta* (how to deal with doubtful matters), the issue of belief is comprised of ten categories. In one of the ten, **Buddha stated one should not believe in written manuals or Holy Scriptures.** This implies Buddha instructed the use of balance as well as pros and cons to evaluate the trustworthiness of dhamma. With the proper understanding of cause and effect, decide whether or not to subscribe to a belief. Even if teachings are attributed to Buddha, it is merely a writer's claim. Readers must use careful examination to prevent potential problems in the future.

I will expound on Prince Siddhāttha's ordination as an ascetic. In regards to what actually transpired, I will leave that up to the reader to decide what to believe. This account is derived from the Laotian version, which differs slightly from the Thai rendition. I hope that intellectual readers use their aptitude to realize that some sections are similar, while others differ from the Thai version. The parts that differ are Buddha's history according to the Laotian records. Please understand this accordingly, so that reasonable comparisons can be made.

Life as a Child and Young Adult

According to records from that time, Buddha was five days old when he received a prophecy from eight Brahmin Scholars. Seven of the eight prophesized that if Prince Siddhāttha were to become a ruler, he would be a mighty king. If he were to ordain as an ascetic he would become a Buddha, supreme in the three realms. He would bring dhamma to the people, and many would become *arriyapuggala*, attain ultimate emancipation, and enter nirvana. The seven Brahmins predicted similar occurrences and confirmed that Prince Siddhāttha would fall under the dual prophecy with certainty. However the eighth Brahmin, the young Kondanna, analyzed the *puggala* characteristics of Prince Siddhāttha and pointed a single finger upward. He prophesized, **"Prince Siddhāttha will not be a world monarch. He will unequivocally ordain and attain enlightenment as a Buddha."**

Upon receiving the prophecies, King Suddhodana felt uneasy as he had aspirations for his son to continue rule as a royal King. In the following period, as his son grew older, he sent him to be educated at Takkasilā with the teacher Wisawamit. Once he completed his courses on Tiveda and eighteen curriculums on royal governance, he returned to Kapilavastu. He was sixteen years of age, a teenager. His father was extremely worried, constantly reminded of the prophecy of the Brahmin Kondanna, in which his son would not be a world monarch. So he plotted to enchant Prince Siddhāttha with earthly behaviors. Eventually, King Suddhodana figured that as a teen, the presence of beautiful women would steer thoughts of ordination far from Prince Siddhāttha's mind. Thus, the king constructed palaces and arranged for attractive young maidens to tend to his every need, both day and night. There were performances of dance, song, and music from a plethora of instruments. Bliss and enjoyment reigned throughout both day and night. There were sixty thousand beautiful women for him to choose from. Prince Siddhāttha enjoyed himself according to the King's plan to enrapture him in worldly pleasures. Three palaces were constructed for each season- hot, rainy, and cold. These were all encompassed in the King's plan, of which Prince Siddhāttha was unaware.

Then, King Suddhodana arranged a marriage between Prince Siddhāttha and Princess Yaṡodharā. The King hoped that an heir would soon be born to his son, and he would be completely enthralled with his wife and son. Thus the saying,

"Puttagīvā

A child as a trap around the neck,

Dhanapāda

Worldly possessions tied to the leg as an anchor,

Bhariyāhattha

A spouse as a rope pulling on the wrist. Whoever can undo these three traps will be liberated from *samasāra*"

The king was convinced that these three traps would be certain to tie down the prince. Each night and each day, Prince Siddhāttha would be pleased with the world, while remaining completely unaware. The king continued to plot to build palace walls that were thick and strong. There would be four entrances, each with three gates. Each gate required the strength of eight people to be capable of opening or closing. There were two hundred guards per entrance. Each of them worked for the king, guarding the palace and especially Prince Siddhāttha. Specific and definite instructions were given: Whichever corresponding door the prince used to venture out on his own would be the one in which all those guards would be executed. Mandates were to come from the king, his father, only. Guards were to stand on duty twenty four hours of the day. This method was used to prevent prince Siddhāttha from leaving the palace walls. Calling it a VIP prison would not be inaccurate. If things transpired according to plan, Prince Siddhāttha would not ordain as an ascetic. When the king aged, Prince Siddhāttha would assume the throne. Under these circumstances, Prince Siddhāttha was completely unaware of his father's plans. At this time there was no cause or reason that would indicate how Prince Siddhāttha would be ordained. Many years passed and Princess Yaśodharā gave birth to a son named Rahula.

From here on out, be alert and use reason for contemplation because this version of the Buddha's history is derived from the Laotian renditions. The Laotian Buddha's history which I will begin explaining will differ slightly from the Thai version. However, it will share some points with the Thai account. I will describe both of them in parallel in order for the story to be complete and rich with cause and effect.

Given that the king, by building a palace

and prolonging the time, found a way to prevent the prince from ordaining, you all must pay careful attention to discover the true cause behind his ordination. Thus far, the prince had visited his father once a month. Before each visit, a messenger would be sent beforehand to inform the king of the prince's intent to visit. Only when the king permitted, would the visit commence as planned. Each visit would be taken with either a small or large group, but always with Princess Yaṡodharā's accompaniment. The king would send a message to inform the guards of Prince Siddhāttha's plan to visit him. Under no other circumstances were the gates to be opened for the prince to venture out on his own. The king, fearing that Prince Siddhāttha would escape and ordain as an ascetic, used his authority to enforce this.

Visit to Kapilavastu

Once the prince reached twenty nine years of age, it was during this very period that the merit and *pāramī* that he had cultivated met with his aspiration to become a Buddha. One day, Prince Siddhāttha paid his father a royal visit to ask for permission to visit Kapilavastu and see how the people lived. Since his birth, he had never seen the city of Kapilavastu. At this point, the king was troubled and afraid his son would be exposed to undesirable sights. He might even become jaded from those sights and his mindset might veer towards ordination. The king responded, "My Prince Siddhāttha, I am not prepared for this visit to Kapilavastu. When I am ready, I will send you a message." Prince Siddhāttha, Princess Yaśodharā, and their court returned to their palace. During this time, King Suddhodana was filled with anxiety and concern. Since Prince Siddhāttha resolved to visit Kapilavastu, there would be repercussions if the king refused permission. Thus, the king delayed his reply. King Suddhodana then called a meeting of his council and councilors. He relayed to them the story of how Prince Siddhāttha asked to visit Kapilavastu in order to facilitate discussion. There was unanimous agreement that it would be appropriate for Prince Siddhāttha to go. This was justified by his age and the fact that he already had a wife and a son. In addition to palaces that afforded a multitude of comforts, he was also enraptured in possessions, status, praises, and sensual pleasures. It was unlikely he had entertained the thought of ordaining as an ascetic. Everyone agreed it would be suitable for Prince Siddhāttha to visit Kapilavastu.

From that point, King Suddhodana sought advice from his council about the manner in which the visit would transpire. What would be a suitable course? Everyone agreed that the pathway must be attractive, with an abundance of flowers and flags waving at every location, because there would be many people in the procession. It was subsequently announced to all the people in each county within the borders of Kapilavastu that collaboration was needed to give the streets a facelift for Prince Siddhāttha's visit. People received the news and came from all areas to assist in the efforts. Because everyone was happy and willing to help out, the beautification of the pathway was completed rapidly. Arrangements were made according to caste- King, Brahmin, Vessa, and Sudda- as suitable. The old and the sick had a separate area coordinated to welcome the prince. A brick tunnel with holes was fashioned. Everyone was to stay within the tunnel to view Prince Siddhāttha, Princess Yaśodharā, Rahula, and their followers. Once everything was organized and orderly, King Suddhodana sent a message to Prince Siddhāttha stating the date and time of the visit arranged for Prince Siddhāttha, Princess Yaśodharā, Rahula, and their followers. This was also formally announced to every single one of the countless residents of Kapilavastu. On this particular day, what will happen to Prince

Siddhāttha? Pay careful attention in order to understand the origination of Prince Siddhāttha's decision to ordain as an ascetic.

Upon the set date, masses of people hailing from every town, village, and county came to receive the prince. The official designated police and soldiers put forth every effort into orchestrating a warm welcome according to King Suddhodana's specifications. For the old, ailing, or weak, walking amongst the crowds could result in a loss of life. Thus, a separate arrangement was made for these people. Since Prince Siddhāttha's birth, the people had never laid eyes on him nor Princess Yaśodharā. Everyone awaited the arrival of the three without a blink of the eye. When it was time, Prince Siddhāttha, Princess Yaśodharā, and Rahula arrived in a decorated and fragrant vehicle. Soldiers, personal servants, and courtesans followed closely. The procession was immensely beautiful and the crowd raised their hands in the lotus position. Without missing a single beat, they continuously and loudly bellowed in a resonating unison, "Saddhu, Saddhu." This was a historical moment for the human beings in that era. Wherever the procession arrived, there were people with hands raised in the lotus position chanting, "Saddhu, Saddhu."

Now comes the point of paramount importance. The old and ailing were crowded within the tunnel, with an insufficient number of peepholes. People fought, pulling on one another, for a chance at a viewing. The weak, due to their old age, and the sick, who were already weakened from their conditions, both wanted to participate in the viewing like everyone else. So they climbed on top of other people in order to see, and when their strength gave out they fell, turning into a ladder for others to step on for a viewing. They were already weak and sick, and to add insult to injury, people were literally crushing and trampling on them. People died in droves. Those with sufficient energy ascended to the top of the human ladder, while those who were already in the process of viewing would not give up their spots. They yelled at each other and the loud resonance escaped from the tunnel, "I want to see, too! I want to see, too!" There was a thunderous clash from the dichotomic sounds of "Saddhu, Saddhu" and "I want to see, too! I want to see, too!" As the *devas* had intended, the reverberation of, "I want to see, too! I want to see, too!" traveled to the prince's ear. The sounds did not disappear. Prince Siddhāttha did not know who the resonance, "I want to see, too! I want to see, too!" belonged to, nor what it was that they desired to see. He asked Channa, "Channa, this sound which I am hearing, 'I want to see, too! I want to see, too!' Who are they and what do they want to see?" Channa replied, "This is the sound of the elderly and the ailing, who have been separated into the tunnel. Everyone wants to get a good look at you, and there aren't enough viewing holes in that crowded space. That is why they are yelling, 'I want to see, too! I want to see, too!'" Once Prince Siddhāttha heard Channa's reply, he responded, "I came today to see Kapilavastu and for its people to see me."

Prince Siddhāttha ordered the police and soldiers who were keeping the peace to fashion a pathway. "I am going into the tunnel. I came on this visit so that everyone could see me. It is not acceptable to block out these people." Then Prince Siddhāttha and Channa entered the tunnel. Once inside the tunnel, **the Prince was shocked at the striking dichotomy[1]. He experienced a solemn awakening and empathized with all those people. He had seen with his own eyes, the old, ailing, and dead, all in one place.**

---

[1] The dichotomy between the attractive and young people and the old, sick, and dead people in the tunnel was stunningly evident. Prior to the Kapilavastu visit, the two were intermingled, undifferentiated, and were considered normal. During the visit, the physical separation made the dichotomic reality obvious, and the Prince was able to see the truth of the world.

Encountering the Four Divine Messengers

At that moment, The king of *Devas* ordered Phra Visanukamma from the *deva* world to appear as a meditating ascetic in that area. The prince clearly saw, and was the only one able to see, this vision. **Prince Siddhāttha's seeing the old, ailing, dead, and ascetic all in one place, is called the four divine messengers.** Once he encountered the four messengers, he guarded his emotions and appeared composed, as he was a Prince. Even back at the vehicle, the Prince put on a calm facade in order to hide his true thoughts from his wife and followers. The vision the prince had experienced stood out in his mind at all times. At the completion of the Kapilavastu visit, the prince returned to his palace. All his life, he had never reflected on the old, ailing, or dead. With each day and night, he had been consumed with worldly sense pleasures.

Once back at the palace, he guarded his thoughts such that Princess Yaṡodharā could not catch on. There was one thing that was out of place. He did not visit the courtesans to delight in their dancing and musical compositions as was customary. But this was not given a second thought, as it was assumed the prince was physically and mentally fatigued. He just needed some time to rest. His speech was not as cheerful nor did he smile as usual. Princess Yaṡodharā and the courtesans did not know what had caused this to happen.

There was one other unconventional thing. Once the prince awakened from his sleep, he would customarily walk to and fro. In this period, the prince deliberated over the images of the old, ailing, and dead people in order to revive his memory. In the past, the prince had seen old, sick, and dead people, but considered it to be normal and did not think much of it. But this time, the prince could not help but think about these things. He continued to reflect upon what he had seen. He knew that it was more than common that people aged, got sick, and died. The prince further probed this matter to investigate whether there was a way for people to prevent aging, sickness, and death. There must be a solution. It was likened to how day must accompany night and cold was the opposite of hot. These were things that could cancel each other out. Thus birth, aging, sickness, and death must also have a method of cancellation. The prince thought about this and considered it for quite a bit.

The prince delved deeper. Considering that humans have been born, what is the cause for human birth? It was in this very quandary that the prince could not find an answer. He expended considerable effort searching for the answer. During that time, the prince realized that while he saw the old, ailing, and dead, he also saw an ascetic sitting in peaceful meditation. "If I were an ascetic in a serene and quiet environment, I may be able to know the cause and factors of human birth." That night, the prince felt an irresistible desire to ordain as an ascetic, and he sought out a way to do so.

That night, it was late and hushed, there was a pregnant moon radiating a brilliant bright light and a tender breeze lightly wafting through the leaves and blades of grass. The flowers adorning the palace fluttered gently from time to time. The air was crisp and cold and the fog drifted intermittently with the wind. Stars in the night sky sparkled, while lights twinkled when kissed by moonbeams. Dew drops dripped from leaves, and crickets and cicada sounded an interwoven melody. The leaves in the forest within the palace quivered eerily. In the hushed night, Princess Yaṡodharā and Rahula were deep in slumber within the palace. The room was dimly lit, as Princess Yaṡodharā cradled Rahula in her chest, unaware of what was to transpire in this night. Prince Siddhāttha slowly walked up to the room in which Princess Yaṡodharā was sleeping. He reached out his arm and tenderly opened the door. He glanced over towards the bed and saw Princess Yaśodharā and Rahula were sound asleep. So he bid them a silent final farewell.

"My dear Princess Yaśodharā, Rahula. In this night, I bid you farewell. In the past, we blissfully slept beside one another, never once upset. You are not to blame for my circumstance. On this night, I will leave you in order to ordain as an ascetic. If I attain enlightenment as a Buddha, I will visit you. If I do not become a Buddha, I bid you farewell in death. Princess Yaśodharā, Rahula, my infant son, I bid you farewell tonight. I will not return. I bid you farewell, my love."

Ordination as an Ascetic

Prince Siddhāttha walked away slowly, feeling fainter with each step. He turned his face to look at the flickering light in the bedroom of Princess Yaṡodharā and Rahula. He felt such pity for Princess Yaṡodharā and Rahula. He sighed heavily and tears welled up. He was practically unable to take another step. He walked out to see Channa, and called for him in a light whisper, "Channa, Channa. Wake up. I have pressing business I am leaving for tonight, and I am in a hurry. Quickly, put the saddle on Kataka and take me out of the palace immediately." Channa awoke and without washing his face he arranged the saddle. Prince Siddhāttha immediately mounted the horse, Kataka. In that moment, Kataka neighed vociferously three times, the piercing sounds resonating in every direction. Typically, Kataka's neighs reverberated as far as eight *yojana* (a distance of approximately eighty miles).

Everyone everywhere would hear the sound and would be awakened from their slumber. That night it was a true marvel that people slept, oblivious. It was attributed to the *devas'* intentions and the *pāramī* (the ten perfections) of Prince Siddhāttha that dictated he would ordain in this night. Prince Siddhāttha tugged on Kataka's reigns and directed him to the gate on the east side. He sat atop Kataka, who trotted slowly while Channa walked beside him. He did not know what the prince's business was or how he would get out. The colossal gates were shielded by at least three additional layers of gigantic gates. Each gate could only be opened or closed by eight men, and up to two hundred of King Suddhodana's soldiers stood guard. The *pāramī* of Prince Siddhāttha along with the assistance of *devas* compelled the night guards to sleep soundly and unaware. The large gate miraculously swung open on its own. Once Prince Siddhāttha, riding atop of Kataka, and Channa passed, the gates miraculously shut again. It was as if nothing had transpired. The night guards awakened completely oblivious.

The next morning, the courtesans and servants noticed that something was out of place. This was because the sun was already halfway on its course and Prince Siddhāttha still had not stepped out. So they went to visit Princess Yaṡodharā to inform her that in this morning, Prince Siddhāttha had not been seen leaving his bedroom. Princess Yaṡodharā wondered if something had happened to him. She then walked to his bedroom, opened the door, peeked in, and saw and empty bed. She didn't know which palace he had slept in. The personal servants and courtesans searched for him in the three palaces and combed through all areas within them. He was nowhere to be found. The night guards, when questioned, did not have a clue either. As the stables that Channa tended were searched, Channa and the horse Kataka were found to be missing. Everyone supposed and agreed that Prince Siddhāttha had left the palace. Tears streamed down Princess Yaṡodharā's face. The courtesans bawled, hugging each other in turmoil. Princess Yaṡodharā held Rahula close to her chest and wept, life practically rushing out of her as she said,

"Oh dear husband, what have I done wrong that you have left me and our young Rahula to suffer like this? Or were you upset over something? Why didn't you let me know? Were you angry or unhappy with me? If I had known, I would have changed to fit your every wish. Oh, why did you hurt me like this? Who will I lean on from now on? Oh, please don't leave me. Don't you feel for our newborn son? Please grant me this."

Prince Siddhāttha arrived at the Anoma river and was ordained as an ascetic in that very location. Details of this are available in textbooks. Once ordained, calling him Siddhāttha Bhikkhu is suitable. From then, he heard that the two *tāpasa* (ascetics) practiced well and were esteemed in the community. So, he studied and practiced following their lead. The two *tāpasa* taught meditation for the sole sake of achieving tranquility. Siddhāttha Bhikkhu thus meditated to the point of tranquility, exactly as the two *tāpasa* instructed. The five *abhiññā* (higher psychic powers), the eight *samāpatti* (meditative attainments), *rūpajhāna* (absorptions of the fine material sphere), and *arūpajhāna* (four absorptions of the formless sphere) were all dexterously achieved and became habitual. Siddāttha Bhikkhu achieved tranquility every single time. While meditating, it was as if the conscious was free of *kilesas* (defilements) and *taṇhā* (greed). When his conscious slipped out of tranquility and into sorrow, he always reverted to thoughts of Princess Yaṡodharā and Rahula. **Siddhāttha Bhikkhu practiced continuous tranquil meditation for a year. There was no indication whatsoever of the emergence of insight or wisdom.**

In past lives Siddhāttha Bhikkhu had accumulated perfect *pāramī*, yet once he reached this meditative tranquility, no insight or wisdom emerged. Presently it is taught that meditative tranquility will cause *paññā* to spontaneously arise. What kind of meditative tranquility is this? When Buddha was still alive, he never taught this to his followers. Or if Buddha actually taught this, could you produce an example of whom he taught? Could you describe to me one person that effectively used this method? This is what is called instruction without regard to the manual. Bhikkhu Siddhāttha practiced meditative tranquility enough to merely see it as an example, as I have already explained. And he rejected this method as one that eliminated *kilesas* and *taṇhā*. This method was neither for purity, nor on the path to enlightenment, nor for the purpose of enlightenment. Bhikkhu Siddhāttha left the two *tāpasa* to search for a new and different method.

Afterwards, Bhikkhu Siddhāttha encountered the five *pañcavaggiya* (the five Bhikkhus) who were searching for him. During that period, Bhikkhu Siddhāttha practiced *dukkarakiriyā* (the practice of austerities, self-mortification) at Dongkasiri mountain. He had refrained from drinking water and eating for forty nine days, such that he was emaciated and barely alive. At that point, he had a *nimitta* (omen, sign) and saw the king of *devas* strumming a three stringed sitar. One string was too loose, producing an unharmonious sound. The second string was too taut, also producing an unpleasant sound. The third string was neither loose nor taut, and the sitar was harmonious. Once Siddhāttha Bhikkhu saw this, he paralleled his practice to the sitar strings. Thus, he realized that his diligence was too taut, and if he continued down this path he would not survive.

From then on, he ceased those actions and returned to regular consumption. The five *pañcavaggiya* were unhappy with this and left him. Siddhāttha Bhikkhu was by himself, and on his own. He had the opportunity to see different methods in various practices, but he knew that none were the correct path. Siddhāttha Bhikkhu still did not know what the correct path was. He continued on his way and because he was fatigued, he rested beneath a *bodhi* (sacred fig) tree by the bank of the Neranjara River. He accepted a milk rice offering from Sujata, and floated the golden tray on the river. He wagered,

"If I am to be enlightened as a Buddha in this life, may this golden tray float up the river. If I am not to be enlightened as a Buddha in this life, may this golden tray float down the river with the current."

Finding the Path to Enlightenment on His Own

Once Bhikkhu Siddhāttha released the golden tray, it immediately travelled against the current. Thus he was injected with a great sense of confidence. He was sure to become a Buddha in this lifetime. This was to be the starting point for a new method of practice. In the past five years, Bhikkhu Siddhāttha had never used insight to contemplate any truths. This was the new beginning of Bhikkhu Siddhāttha's usage of *paññā*. The usage of wisdom in this case was the use of the parallel of the golden tray for consideration. So, understand that the inaugural point of practicing leads off with *paññā*. This is of monumental importance. Continue reading carefully and diligently. There exist obvious reasons confirming this as correct. This mode of practice is completely unlike that which the two *tāpasa* taught. **This inaugural point initiated when Bhikkhu Siddhāttha discovered *sammādiṭṭhi*, rational perception. *Sammāsaṅkappa*, right thought from insight-wisdom and causality,** was consequently righteous and rational.

As Bhikkhu Siddhāttha used the parallel of the floating golden tray for consideration, his mind was able to clearly recognize and understand the foundations of the Three Common Characteristics: *annicca* (impermanence), *dukkha* (suffering), and *anattā* (cessation of existence in the supposed form). Wagering has perpetually walked hand and hand with the human world. One example is lifting a Buddha statue or wagering in some other form. There must always be two resolutions. If something is to happen, then the statue will be able to be lifted up. If it is not to happen, then the statue will not be able to be lifted up. In the same vein, Bhikkhu Siddhāttha also wagered. If he were to become a Buddha, the golden tray would float against the current. If he was not meant to be a Buddha, the golden tray would be carried along in the current. In this situation, the golden tray travelled against the tide, providing Bhikkhu Siddhāttha with confidence in his ability. **The golden tray was employed as a parallel to utilize *paññā* in deliberation. The golden tray traversing against the current was interpreted as Bhikkhu Siddhāttha's own mind. He resolved to use attentive wisdom to train his mind, forbidding it from being pleased and satisfied with the desires surging along with the world's currents. Typically the mind desires easy and effortless delights falling under the five *kāmaguṇa* (sensual pleasures).** The mind is pleased by tangible appearances, sounds, scents, tastes, and delicate sensations. Bhikkhu Siddhāttha had desired these things. But from this point on, he would use *paññā* to resist these pleasures. If the mind was not pleased with these types of things, then incorrect perception and misunderstanding of worldly pleasures would not exist. This is how

Bhikkhu Siddhāttha used discernment to not allow the mind from being pleased or displeased and to reject possessions, status, accolades, and contentment that were chained to worldly sensual pleasures. Bhikkhu Siddhāttha used wisdom to coach his mind to be unattached to these things. He trained himself that these were all things that tied the mind down and created infatuation with and strong attachment to the world.

Discernment Used to Teach Oneself to Acquire Expansive Knowledge

Bhikkhu Siddhāttha used discernment for analysis and also taught and trained his mind to have perpetual, expansive knowledge. This was for the purpose of understanding that all kinds of thoughts arise, stay, and pass. Using discernment for analysis requires both moving in and out according to the situation. For instance, seeing an external occurrence, like seeing people who are old, ailing, and dead. Internalize the parallel: we too will follow that course. Or externalize the parallel such that both internal and external are one and the same: we also age, get sick and die. Whatever occurs to others will similarly occur to us. Others experience suffering, and we too, experience suffering. Other people are uncertain, and so we are uncertain as well. Other people's bodies are *anattā* (not self), and our bodies are *anattā*, ceased from self-being, as well. When experiencing and seeing human corpses in a particular condition, internalize that condition such that we similarly see our own bodies as corpses.

Analyze the past and future in terms of the present. Scrutiny of issues in the past relies on *saññā* (memory), while examination of issues in the future relies on *sammuti* (supposed form). *Saññā* and *sammuti* are crucial supports for *paññā* (insight-wisdom). *Saññā* is memory and is selective in this sense. Elect to remember things that involve *dosa* (destructive consequences) and *bhaya* (peril) so that the mind is scared to encounter them. *Dosa* and *bhaya* exist in this world, and everyone born into this world must experience and encounter them, whether to a small or large degree. Thus, choose to remember things which involve *dosa* and *bhaya* so that the mind does not relapse into pleasureful things. If something conduces *rakataṇhā* (craving fine sense pleasures), lust, or passion and is in the form of tangible appearances, sound, scent, tastes, or delicate sensations- and *paññā* is absent- then there will be infatuation and attachment to these things. Those who possess righteous *paññā* seek only to remember things with *dosa* and *bhaya* in tow, and then use those to develop understanding. One illustration of this is our own physical form and someone else's. Use *paññā* to consider how both these corporal forms conduce *dosa* and *bhaya*. The *dosa* from our own bodies translates to the *dosa* others experience with their bodies as well. All bodies are subject to *lokapaya*, illness or death, which is harmful to life. In past lives, bodies have experienced *dosa* and *bhaya* just like in present lives.

Contemplating the Physical Aggregates

Only those with *paññā* will know and understand, according to the truth, that physical form is not as attractive and pleasant as is perceived. The nature of physical form is not at all attractive, but rather, is filthy. Despite showering to remove dirt, the filthiness of corporal form does not wash away. If one abstains from showering for ten days, the odor of the filth will permeate to the outside. It will be the disgust and revulsion of society. For example, hair on the head, hair on the body, nails, teeth, and skin are all unattractive and have not boasted that they are pleasant in any way. The attractiveness is attributed to *kilesas* (defilements), *saṅkhāra* (imagination), *moha* (delusion), and *avijjā* (absence of knowledge). P hysical form is pleasant because of misunderstandings. It is attractive because of love, pleasure, lust, and passion. If the mind does not possess love, pleasure, lust, and passion, physical form will be devoid of any measure of beauty. This is because beauty is not dependent on physical form in any way. Accessories and adornments are merely a façade, and cosmetics are only intended for pretense. Similarly, corpses are made up with color and design, while within, they are rotting, filthy, and constantly radiating a stench. Likewise, our human physical form, as well as that of others, is adorned with accessories and fragrances to mask the rotting stench of our bodies. This allows humans to live alongside one another.

The use of insight-wisdom for discernment is employed to know the truth, creation, existence, and cessation of the physical form aggregate. This is because the creation of the physical form aggregate does not transpire within a single day. It will gradually develop, and once development is complete, suffering of the mind and body serves as its shadow. Impermanence applies from the state of a red blood cell, to an infant, to a teenager, to an adult, to an aging and sick person, and eventually to a deceased person. Upon death, the physical form aggregate will become *anattā*, the cessation of existence in the supposed form of an 'animal,' 'person,' 'self,' or an 'other.' The conventional perception that physical form belongs to the self will cease. The composition of the four elements (earth, water, air, and fire) that are recognized as the human body will disintegrate back into each of its original elements. This goes along with the basis of *anattā*, which is complete cessation. Unlike that which we perceive, nothing at all belongs to the self.

When the mind lacks wisdom, infatuation and clinging will occur. Once a desire is unfulfilled and different from what was imagined, suffering exists. Desire is only generated in the direction of contentment and pleasure. Birth is desired within a family of riches, status, accolades, and happiness. If all human desires were fulfilled, the state of the human world would not exist as it does. If everyone shared the same condition, no one would be able to criticize another because of the identical possession of riches, status, accolades, and happiness. Or if the world were completely comprised of orphans and the poor, while lacking riches and status, and only contained harsh words, gossip, and constant suffering of the mind and body, no one would want to be born in this human world. Everyone desires happiness.

No one desires the decline of wealth or status, nor gossip, suffering, and unhappiness. Yet, there is no escape because the truth is completely wrapped around this world. It is improbable to select only happiness. There is a need for things that are desired and satisfying to exist permanently. Once these needs are unfulfilled, suffering arises. This is how humans constantly try to resist the truth of nature. Yet there does not exist a single person in this world who is completely satisfied and content. You name it, no one ever fulfills their desires. Once born, everyone must face aging, illness, and death.

The Cause of Birth within the Three Realms

In another angle, Bhikkhu Siddhāttha thought, what if the golden tray floated along with the current? Where would the golden tray end up? Bhikkhu Siddhāttha internalized the parallel of the golden tray, comparing it to his own mind. If the golden tray was carried along with the current, it would continue to float. Whatever direction the current took, the tray would follow. Eventually it would drift out into the vast ocean, floating around without end. Likewise, if the mind was impregnated with *kilesas* (defilements) and *taṇhā* (greed), then the mind would continue to be born and die within the great world of *sammuti* (supposed form) without end. At low tide, the golden tray would temporarily land on sand or an island. At high tide, it would drift along the current without end. In the same vein, love and wants have no end, and the desires of the mind have no boundaries or limits. Thus the phrase,

Natti taṇhā samanati

> **An ocean as vast as *taṇhā* does not exist.**
> **Any amount of water can never fill up the ocean.**
> **Likewise, the mind can never be satisfied in its greed.**

Bhikkhu Siddhāttha thought about when the tray fell onto sand or various islands during low tide. He employed insight and compared it to his mind. The mind fell into a human existence, sometimes born as a King, others as a Brahman, Vessa, Suddha, or Candāla (untouchables). Sometimes it was a birth in a small or large sphere like the sense, form, formless, or animal spheres. Bhikkhu Siddhāttha used insight to contemplate this, and thus emerged *ñāṇatassana*, the wisdom to clearly know and realize the cause of human birth. While he was still Prince Siddhāttha he had seen the elderly, the sick, and the deceased. The cause of these conditions was birth. At that time, he could not determine the cause of birth. He had just discerned the cause of human birth from the parallel of the golden tray. It is ***taṇhā* (greed) that propels rebirth and cycling through the three spheres. These are *kāmataṇhā*, *bhavataṇhā*, and *vibhavataṇhā*.**

1. *Kāmataṇhā* means *vatthukāma* (material desires) and *kilesakāma* (sensuality, lust). *Vatthukāma* means material possessions we are attached to and pleased with. Consider that these possessions belong to the world and are merely relied on, day to day. If these possessions are considered personal belongings, it is only in a legal sense or for the duration of life on earth. But once the *citta* departs from the physical body, the personal belongings lose all meaning and association to the self. Those who are alive assert claims on those belongings accordingly. Likewise, after a couple months or years pass, those people will similarly depart from the possessions. No one can take worldly belongings with them. The phrase, "belongs to me," will become void. Nothing absolutely belongs to the self. If there is attachment and contentment, there will be suffering. Once the mind realizes and understands that physical form and material worldly belongings are merely daily necessities, then the clinging will loosen and the attachment will be of a lesser degree. Greed and misunderstanding will gradually dissolve. This is an illustration of how to eliminate attachment. There must be *sati* and *paññā* to teach the mind to realize the truth. The mind will thus gradually loosen its attachment to desire, which is *taṇhā*, to the point of elimination.

Kilesakāma **means** ***kāmaguṇa*** **(sensual pleasures) the mind is attached to and pleased with.** These are tangible appearances, sounds, scents, tastes, and delicate sensations. The mind possesses love, lust, and passion as emotions. It has a need for these *kāmaguṇa*. And once the mind is fixated on *kāma* (an object of sensual enjoyment), it will urgently direct all efforts towards the quest for *kāma*. The mind's perceived needs, masked by *kilesakāma*, pervasively exist in the world. But, Bhikkhu Siddhāttha employed *sati* and *paññā* to analyze and eradicate misunderstandings and misperceptions, so that the mind clearly realized and understood the *dosa* (destructive consequences) and *bhaya* (peril) that arose from *kāmaguṇa*.

2. *Bhavataṇhā* (craving for sensual pleasures connected with the view of eternalism) refers to the mind's contentment with the realm into which it is born and its aversion to any change. It continues to desire existence in whatever realm it has existed in. If this is a human realm, it will continue to prefer existence in the human realm forever. Despite other's claims of a happier existence in the *deva* or *brahma* worlds, the mind is not at all interested. It desires an existence identical to its current state. Or if is there is reason compelling a departure from its current realm, the mind will be attached to something such as children, grandchildren, or worldly possessions that it is content with.

3. *Vibhavataṇhā* (craving for sensual pleasures connected with the view of nihilism) denotes the mind's not wanting to be reborn into a realm it is dissatisfied with. For example, those who exist in the formless world do not desire rebirth in the human realm. Those humans born into wealth, a highly regarded status and a pleasing abundance of *kāmaguṇa* (sensual pleasures) do not desire birth in an impoverished family. They also do not yearn for a birth as a cripple, or to be missing an ear or an eye, somehow physically incomplete. Nor is there an aspiration for birth in the *apāyabhūmi* (the four planes of loss and woe). These four realms of misery include *niraya* (hell realm), *pittivisaya* (hungry ghost realm), *tiracchānayoni* (animal realm), and *asurakāya* (demon realm). Even though a birth in these realms is not desired, it is warranted as a result of bad karma. There is no right to demand a rebirth to satisfy a desire. Karma that is committed dictates the bearing of the next realm of rebirth.

These three *taṇhā* are the cause and catalysts for the cycling of rebirth in the Three Realms (*kāmaloka*: the world of sense desire, *rūpaloka*: form-sense sphere, and *arūpaloka*: formless, immaterial sphere). Once the cause is exterminated, the issue of rebirth in the Three Realms is eradicated. The perception that *taṇhā* generates happiness is a personal misunderstanding.

Unavoidable Suffering

Unavoidable suffering is the condition of anguish particular to the *khanda*, aggregates. Even if a person is wealthy and pleased by an abundance of *kāmaguṇa*, the condition of suffering will always manifest in the aggregates. For example, the form aggregate in which the mind resides manifests suffering in the body and mind. Although no one desires this affliction, it is unavoidable because of its natural course. Despite exhaustive efforts to eliminate suffering, it cannot be accomplished. For instance, the quest for *kāmaguṇa* (tangible appearances, sounds, scents, tastes, and delicate sensations) can obscure suffering. but no one can completely suppress it. This is because suffering is an absolute truth corresponding to the form aggregate. It reveals itself at all times, day and night. Whether standing, walking, sitting, or sleeping, these are merely postures that temporarily circumvent suffering. None of these postures are neither permanently nor certainly painless. Standing, walking, sitting, or sleeping for prolonged periods causes suffering.

Where will we find happiness from the form aggregate? At last, tangible appearances, sounds, scents, tastes, and delicate sensations put a temporary veil over suffering. Instead of producing positive consequences, it incites increased and more pronounced suffering. Similarly, putting out a fire with sawdust and rice hulls precisely stimulates the flame instead of extinguishing it. Once the fire grows again, duplicating the action of throwing in sawdust and rice hulls is not an intelligent method at all. Likewise, using tangible appearances, sounds, scents, tastes, and delicate sensations to eliminate the mind's anguish, only serves to mask the suffering. It is only a means of temporary relief from suffering. Eventually the *āyatana* (sense-objects) will transform into an efficient cause of suffering. This is because the experience of *āyatana* causes happiness and unhappiness, and feeds the flame of *raka* (desire for delicate sense pleasures), *tossa* (anger), and *moha* (delusion). Thus, Buddha stated, not controlling the eyes, ears, nose, tongue, body, and mind so that they don't travel outward and become intertwined with physical form, sound, scent, taste, sensation, and emotions, is the precise cause of suffering for the mind. Therefore suffering arises and paves the way for other types of unintended suffering to congregate as the mind's misery. Please consider this using *paññā* (insight-wisdom) in order to clearly realize and see the truth as it is.

As for aging, sickness, and death that evoke suffering, these are things that are unavoidable. No matter how terrified of them, there is no escape because birth has already occurred. Aging, sickness, and death are consequences of birth. If birth can be ceased, then suffering within the Three Realms will never develop. Therefore, those practitioners who do not desire birth and suffering must analyze birth and suffering during this lifetime. This must be done so as to gradually extinguish the attachment to future lives. This will cut off the momentum of anxious concern, which serves as a catalyst for rebirth, through the use of razor sharp and daring concentration and discernment, to the point of ***anālayo*** (the extinction of caring and attachment to anything in the world). The site for rebirth will be destroyed and the root cause which spawns rebirth will be extinguished. Thus the saying,

Samulang taṇhāng apuyaha

Therefore, being one who uproots taṇhā and destroys all its minor roots,

Nicchato parinibhuddo

the mind absolutely ceases wanting and extinguishes kilesas and dukkha

Once Bhikkhu Siddhāttha considered *saccadhamma* (the truth) using continuous insight, his mind realized and understood in alignment with the truth. Similar to shining a light in a dark place, once the bright light shines in any direction, the eye sees objects and knows what they are. Likewise, once the mind has the bright shining light of wisdom, the mind sees and accurately knows the *saccadhamma* for what it is. It sees *dukkha* (suffering) as *dukkha*. It sees impermanent objects as *anicca* (impermanence). It sees the state of *anattā* as *anattā* (cessation of existence in supposed form). If the mind truly sees and understands according to these truths, the mind sees and understands the truth correctly.

The Emergence of Buddha's Wisdom

Ñāṇatassana emerged in Bhikkhu Siddhāttha's mind. Righteous perception and understanding according to the truths of the world expanded without bounds. Any one thing has a cause for its occurring, exists for a period, and ceases when its cause ceases. Nothing can exist permanently. Regardless of whether or not that thing is possessed by a soul, everything falls under impermanence. But humans refuse to accept this impermanence and suffer as a consequence. We do not want things to depart and disappear from us. We want our possessions to stay with us forever, so we become attached and believe that those items actually belong to us. Once the state of those belongings transform, suffering arises. Thus, the mind suffers because of what we possess. **If the mind believes that it possesses an object, it will suffer because of that object.** *Taṇhā* (greed) is attached to and involved with impermanent objects. But, we want those objects to be permanent. Money, gold, or belongings that appear in this world are merely earthly belongings since the dawn of the world's existence. They are only intended for daily use, for the purpose of day to day survival. The days, months, and years that follow will see a transformation in the state of those things. Those lacking wisdom are not able to understand this concept and consequently suffer because of worldly possessions. If the mind is still pleased with, attached to, worried about, and caring for worldly belongings and the five sense pleasures, then the mind will cling to, believe in, and be reborn in this world without end.

Bhikkhu Siddhāttha used wisdom to consider the truth as such, and *sammādiṭṭhi* (righteous realization and understanding of the truth) arose in his mind. Bhikkhu Siddhāttha then assured himself that this method was correct. The method was discovered through his own wisdom. No one was his instructor, nor did he find the path in a manual. This is because the truths in the world already exist as the manual for training, but it is due to a deficiency in wisdom that these truths are not discerned. Examples that are *saccadhamma*, the truth, are ubiquitous in this world. Bhikkhu Siddhāttha thus stated, **"Take a needle point and stick it in any location in the world, *saccadhamma* will exist in that location."** Without wisdom, sitting or sleeping on top of the truth or stepping back and forth on it will not elucidate that *saccadhamma* in any way. Thus the phrase,

Natthi paññā samaābhaā

There does not exist a light as bright as wisdom

Wisdom in this sense means *tassanañāṇa*, which is different from *ñāṇatassana*. *Tassanañāṇa* means realization before understanding. *Ñāṇatassana* means understanding before realization.

Both of these *ñāṇa* must work together simultaneously for a resultant product to occur. For example, once one understands, one must realize. If one solely understands with the absence of realization, one will not have the courage to decide what is correct or incorrect. It is possible that misunderstanding will occur. If one realizes and does not understand, then one cannot define what was realized. One will similarly be unable to decide what is correct or incorrect. Therefore, *ñāṇatassana* and *tassanañāṇa* must be defined in terms of cause and effect. For example, from understanding *saccadhamma* through manuals, one will only be able to speak according to manuals. The real truth will not be realized. Or if one realizes according to *saccadhamma* (the truth) without understanding that what it realized was the truth, then the realization is without benefit. The process of making a decision will be uncertain.

Likewise, those who fish and reach down into the water only to grab a snake's head, while believing it to be a fish, are delighted at the aspect of catching a fish. This is because only understanding is present. So a decision may possibly be incorrect because there is an understanding that it is a fish that was caught. Once the hand grasping the object is above water and one realizes that the object is in fact a snake, the understanding of the object as a fish will disappear. This is because the truth of its being a snake will be realized. The way to prevent a snake bite will thus be elementary. In regards to the truth, realizing before understanding or understanding before realizing lies in the same vein. Buddha stated,

Asādhammo sannatthanō

***Saccadhamma* is ancient and has existed since ancient times**

Saccadhamma has existed alongside the world since its inception. Delusion and infatuation with the world is due to the lack of wisdom to discern *saccadhamma*, which exists in the world.

The Buddha was the one to discover *saccadhamma* before any other in this world. He used *paññā* (insight-wisdom) to analyze these *saccadhamma* and consequently completely detached himself from misperceptions, misunderstandings and delusions. Many months transpired before arriving at this point. During that time, Bhikkhu Siddhāttha practiced continuous diligence. He floated the golden tray in October and used it as an internalized parallel, as was previously detailed. If practice initiates with *sammādiṭṭhi*, then the use of parallels to contemplate other issues is simple.

If the question arises, as to whether or not Bhikkhu Siddhāttha practiced meditation during that period, the answer will be that concentration existed in his mind, but it was focused concentration. As for tranquil meditation, Bhikkhu Siddhāttha had experienced that with the two *tāpasa*. His practice during that time did not develop in any sense. At this time, Bhikkhu Siddhāttha employed focused concentration to boost his wisdom. This focused concentration for the purpose of advancing wisdom does not require repetition of a meditative phrase. Because focused concentration already exists, merely use wisdom in concert. This alert and focused concentration is called *sammādhi,* or concentration meditation. The use of thoughts to contemplate *saccadhamma* according to the truth is called *paññā* (wisdom). *Sati* is the mindful realization of the wisdom used to analyze each issue. Therefore, *sati, sammādhi,* and *paññā* work as a team. The absence of one will result in an imperfect practice.

At this time, Bhikkhu Siddhāttha possessed *sati, sammādhi,* and *paññā*, and his practice of dhamma moved forward by leaps and bounds. *Magga magga ñāṇatassana visuti* (insight to realize and understand the path wholesomely) emerged and thus Bhikkhu Siddhāttha's examples of practice developed wholesomely. In reaching *vimutti nibbāna* (deliverance and enlightenment), perfect *vipassanāñāṇa* (knowing by insight) emerged within Bhikkhu Siddhāttha and he was thus *logavitu*, completely and clearly knowing the world. Thus,

Natthi loke rahonāma

Secrets do not exist in the Three Realms

Within *kāmaloka* (desire realm), *rūpaloka* (form realm), and *arūpaloka* (formless realm), there is no part in these Three Realms that can even begin to mask the Buddha's *vipassanāñāṇa*. Other insight also emerged within the Buddha, like *abhiññā* (supernormal, higher psychic powers).

Abhiññā

Abhiññāñāṇa is insight that arises from direct mental sensation as a result of *sammādhi* (concentration). According to the *pāramī* each individual has cultivated, those who did not train in terms of *abhiññā* (superknowledges, higher psychic powers) in previous lifetimes will not develop *abhiññā* in this lifetime regardless of the amount of tranquil meditation practiced. As for those who have trained in *abhiññā* in past lives, any amount of tranquil meditation will trigger the emergence of *abhiññā*.

Abhiññā can occur with lay people or arriyapuggala (noble persons), regardless of ethnicity, race, or religion. *Abhiññā* can also emerge in people who do not follow any religion. This is because tranquil meditation is universal and has existed along with the world. According to history, before Buddhism arose in the world, there existed those who practiced tranquil meditation and experienced *abhiññā*. As an example, Asita *tāpasa* was well versed in tranquil meditation and *abhiññā*. He visited Prince Siddhāttha a few days after his birth. Also in attendance were Alara *tāpasa* and Utaka *tāpasa*, who taught Bhikkhu Siddhāttha the methods of tranquil meditation. These *tāpasa* were unversed in neither the five nor eight precepts.

There are many types of *abhiññā*. I will briefly explain.

1. *Chakkhuñāṇa* is the divine eye that arises directly from the mind. Whatever is desired to be seen can be viewed by focusing the mind. For example, if desired, the community of *devas* and how their daily lives transpire can be viewed in its entirety. Similarly, the community and lives of those in *niraya* (hell realm) or *pittivisaya* (hungry ghost realm) can be seen.

2. *Sotañāṇa* is the divine ear that makes it possible to hear the sounds from all levels of *devas* along with the tormenting sounds of those in *niraya*.

3. *Cetopariyañāṇa* is the ability to penetrate and know the thoughts of others, whether the thoughts are good or bad. This is telepathy, knowing the status of other's minds.

4. *Iddhividhiñāṇa* is magical powers to dive into or soar above the earth. Both lay people and arriyapuggala have been documented to have this power.

5. *Manomayiddhiñāṇa* is the power of the mind. If desired one person can be multiplied into many persons or a person can transform into animal form.

6. *Pubbenivāsānussatiñāṇa* is the ability to recollect one's former lives, how that life transpired, and who were one's relatives.

7. *Cutūpapātañāṇa* is the knowledge of the deceased, the location of their souls, what karma they are serving, and what will transpire once that karma has been fulfilled.

8. *Attidhungsañāṇa* is the knowledge of the past concerning every issue.

9. *Anakadhungsañāṇa* is the knowledge of the future concerning every issue.

The *abhiññāñāṇa* described here are of the *loki* (worldly) level. They occur only with those who trained in that way during past lives. These various *ñāṇa* (insight) do not in any way eliminate *kilesas* (defilements) or *taṇhā* (greed) from the mind. For those who do not possess wisdom, these *ñāṇa* will create tremendous *kilesas* and *māna attā* (self-conceit) for the self. There will be infatuation and delusion of the self as both grand and good. *Māna attā* will greatly inflate the ego.

During our times, people who possess these kinds of *ñāṇa* are highly regarded and praised by the masses as someone who practices to the fullest extent of righteousness and correctness. Or they may even be admired as an *arahant* who has emerged in the world. If *abhiññāñāṇa* has already occurred to oneself, one must constantly use wisdom to remind oneself that *abhiññāñāṇa* is only for amusement. Do not fall into the belief that one possesses any kind of virtue because it is only a *ñāṇaloki* (worldly insight) that may deteriorate and is in no way permanent. Bhikkhu Siddhāttha possessed the aforementioned *abhiññāñāṇa* before he became enlightened. Yet, he was still an ordinary person and he was unimpressed by these *ñāṇa* in any way.

Āsavakkhayañāṇa Occurs

At the time Bhikkhu Siddhāttha floated the golden tray at the Neranjara River, it was the rainy season and the water level was high. Because of this, he had not yet crossed the river. The following year, once the water level of the Neranjara River fell, Bhikkhu Siddhāttha was able to cross the river. There, he practiced dhamma on the shore containing the Bodhi tree that shared his birthday.

On the night of a full moon in June, the day Buddha was enlightened, he requested hay from a Brahmin. He laid it underneath the Bodhi tree so that he could sit down. It was during this time that *āsavakkhayañāṇa* occurred. Before enlightenment, Bhikkhu Siddhāttha had already experienced all the *ñāṇa*. During the night of his enlightenment there would only be one *ñāṇa* called, ***āsavakkhayañāṇa*, the knowledge that the worldly defilements would cease only within**

a *jalimakajit* (likened to a quick snap of lightning or snap of the fingers).

Āsavakkhayañāṇa is commonly defined in texts as the *ñāṇa* that causes all *āsava* (mental intoxication or defilements) to cease. This causal definition does not have a strong enough foundation to be believable. Once *āsavakkhayañāṇa* arises nothing needs to be done because it is complete and whole process within itself. *Āsavakkhayañāṇa* will not endure for long before enlightenment as a Buddha occurs. This is because *āsavakkhayañāṇa* is a *ñāṇa* that is both brave and powerful. It is a *ñāṇa* (insight) that worldly defilements will cease. Take notice that when Bhikkhu Siddhāttha sat on the stack of hay he had the aspiration, **"I will sit in this place until I become a Buddha. If I do not become enlightened I will forever sit in this place, even if my skin, bones, and muscles deteriorate."**

This signifies that *āsavakkhayañāṇa* had already arisen in Bhikkhu Siddhāttha, and that is why he was brave enough to articulate this aspiration. Beforehand, he had sat in many places without ever uttering these words. This time, Bhikkhu Siddhāttha already knew that all *āsava* would be extinguished. What is more, this kind of aspiration is only an emphasis for those who will champion *āsava* anyway. It is not that the aspiration itself will aid in extinguishing all *āsava*, because they would cease and he would become a Buddha, even without the aspiration.

In texts, Buddha's enlightenment is commonly described as occurring during the full moon in the month of June. His enlightenment started with:

Paṭhamayāma (the first watch - 6:00 to 10:00 pm)

> *Pubbenivāsānussatiñāṇa* (reminiscence of past or previous births) occurs

Majjhimayāma (the middle watch - 10:00 pm to 2:00 am)

> *Cutūpapātañāṇa* (the knowledge of the deceased and the rebirth of beings) occurs

Pacchimayāma (the last watch - 2:00 to 6:00 am)
Āsavakkhayañāṇa (the knowledge that all mental intoxications will be destroyed) occurs

In terms of dhamma practice, I will provide my personal opinion about *pubbenivāsānussatiñāṇa* and *cutūpapātañāṇa*. Both of these *ñāṇa* are *lokiya* (worldly) and should not be grouped with the *lokuttarañāṇa* (insight that is transcendental, beyond these worlds) involved in the night Buddha was enlightened. This is because *āsavakkhayañāṇa* is the *ñāṇa* (insight) of the definite extinguishment of *āsava*. Thus, it is does not make sense for *āsavakkhayañāṇa* to be grouped with the other two. According to the texts, during the three watches *paṭhamayāma*, *majjhimayāma*, and *pacchimayāma*, *pubbenivāsānussatiñāṇa*, *cutūpapātañāṇa* and *āsavakkhayañāṇa* occurred, respectively. In terms of practice, the two worldly *ñāṇa* (*pubbenivāsānussatiñāṇa* and *cutūpapātañāṇa*) were in no way involved in the night of Buddha's enlightenment. Because texts say otherwise, the common interpretation has followed. Consider how Bhikkhu Siddhāttha laid the hay down underneath the Bodhi tree, sat, and articulated his aspiration. All of this indicates that *āsavakkhayañāṇa* had already occurred. It is not suitable to combine the other two worldly *ñāṇa* (*pubbenivāsānussatiñāṇa* and *cutūpapātañāṇa*) with *āsavakkhayañāṇa* (transcendental insight of the cessation of *āsava*). This is only a personal opinion. In order to determine whether or not it is correct, one should use reason as opposed to believing everything in the texts. Otherwise, one will be a *kalamachon*, one who believes in things without using thought or reason.

Āsavakkhayañāṇa only occurs to the *arahant*: 1. Buddha, 2. Paccekabuddha, 3. The *arahant* disciples of Buddha. The term 'enlightenment' is used only with Buddha and Paccekabuddha. The terms 'attain' and 'achieve' are used with disciples: *sotapanna* (one who has achieved the first stage of holiness or steam entry), *sakadagami* (one who has attained the second stage on the path to emancipation and will be reborn only once before final emancipation), and *anagami* (one who achieved the third stage of holiness, a non-returner). Those who are evolved in *vipassanā* (insight development, introspection) may also attain holiness and become arriyapuggala. Those well evolved in *vipassanāñāṇa*, which is wisdom of a higher level, will be able to achieve final emancipation as an *arahant*. This is because *vipassanāñāṇa* is a brave and powerful *ñāṇa* that can be linked with *āsavakkhayañāṇa* (the *ñāṇa*, insight, that *āsava* will cease in a short time). Achievement of each level of arriyapuggala (*sotapanna*, *sakadagami*, *anagami*) is a personal knowledge called *paccatang*. This cannot be compared to or measured against any texts or any person. Even if Buddha is present, it is not necessary to ask what level one has achieved. This individual knowledge is already known. This is the way of those who have achieved *arahantship* in the era of Buddha.

In present times, however, practitioners await approval from teachers to certify which level has been attained. Alternatively, the symptoms and characteristics that one possesses are held up against those described in texts. When there is a perceived match, one draws the conclusion and self-certifies the attainment of each level. In most cases, there is a misperception of the self. If the master's self-certification is discussed with followers (who already have incredible faith in their master) they will, in turn, agree and recertify the master. In most cases during current times, those who are believed to be arriyapuggala have been certified by their followers. Thus, from this, a business transaction with mutual benefit has arisen.

Discernment of Noble Persons is Difficult

In regards to the question of whether or not arriyapuggala of various levels and *arahants* exist in current times, the response is that these individuals do exist. Although few in number, they still exist. Thus the saying,

Aranhanta asuññaloko

> **If those who practice according to *sammādiṭṭhi* still exist, the world will not experience a shortage of the *arahant***

However, those people will not expose themselves to anyone. They will pursue lives as other common ascetics. What this means is that the deportment of past births will be the outward behaviors in the present life. Thus the discernment of noble persons or an *arahant* is extremely difficult, if not impossible. And listening to their preaching will not clarify this issue because there are manuals describing the expected behaviors of the *arahant*. Observation of actions or manners, both verbal and non-verbal is still inconclusive. Thus, the discernment of noble persons is difficult and these analogies exist:

1. Deep waters-deep shadows
2. Deep waters-shallow shadows
3. Shallow waters-deep shadows
4. Shallow waters-shallow shadows

"Deep waters" indicates those arriyapuggala who have achieved a level of emancipation. "Deep shadows" describes the outward actions of one with good manners. "Shallow waters" means those who have not yet achieved a level of holiness. "Shallow shadows" describes the outward actions of one with bad manners.

If the first and the third pair are taken together, it will be impossible to discern which person is noble. This is because both share good manners and calm deportment. If the second and fourth pair are compared, it will be similarly difficult to discriminate which individual is noble. Therefore, discernment of a noble person is difficult.

Many argue that all arriyapuggala remains will become relics upon death. This is actually incorrect. Only *arahant* remains will become relics. As an example, the Buddha, Paccekabuddha and *arahant* remains become relics, but no one else's. Please understand this. Those who seek out merit commonly desire paying respects and giving alms to *arahants*. These actions are considered to warrant a high level of merit. In terms of sermons, these people also desire to listen to only those which are given by an *arahant*. This corresponds to the historical account of King Pasendi's dream. In one aspect of his dream, **water pots of small and large sizes**

were all sitting in the same area. However, rain only fell into the large water pots, and not at all into the small pots.

The Buddha prophesized that in the distant future, to cultivate merit, the *saddhā* (the faithful) would seek out *arahants*, famous ascetics, or elderly ascetics. Possessions and the four types of necessary sustenance (food, clothing, shelter, medicine) of the *saddhā* will be offered in tremendous and beyond-sufficient quantities. Other ascetics will receive little attention and offerings. This method of giving alms does not contribute to the whole of Buddhism because it does not sustain the majority of *sangha* (monks). More junior ascetics are given little attention and importance. This kind of behavior is clearly illustrated in our current times. This is the tail end of the Buddhist era. Even the ascetics themselves do not behave properly, and the *saddhā* have consequently lost respect for the *sangha*. This is how **people lose faith in Buddhism and the mind discredits dhamma.**

The Buddha's Meditation

As for the question of whether or not the Buddha practiced tranquil meditation before his enlightenment, the answer is that the Buddha possessed *sabbaññutañāṇa* (omniscience). He was able to know and practice in every method. He was whole and perfect in behaviors of *paññāvimutti* (emancipation through insight) and *cetovimutti* (deliverance of the mind). He would use the two types of meditation during relevant times. There are two types of meditation:

1. Alert and focused meditation
2. Tranquil meditation

The Buddha was skilled in these two modes of meditation. He possessed *sabbaññu*, omniscience, in every aspect of realization, understanding, and practice. During the period of meditation with the two *tāpasa* (ascetics), tranquil meditation was the goal. Once he departed from the two *tāpasa*, he rested on the shore of the Neranjara River. He received a milk rice offering from Sujada and floated the golden tray. Then, he started a new mode of practice. This was the focused meditation that was previously described.

When the Buddha desired to rest his mind in serenity, he would alternate between *arupajhāna* (formless meditation or absorption) or *rupajhāna* (form meditation). During times that he desired the use of wisdom, he would exercise focused meditation. Whatever Buddha desired to analyze, he would focus on that issue and use discernment until he was satisfied with the thorough investigation.

As for focused and tranquil meditation, each method of meditation is clarified during the dispensation of the Buddha. Because the character of each disciple was different, Buddha separated the two types of meditation such that they would correspond to each disciple's preference. If meditation corresponds to one's character, one's practice will quickly evolve. You will understand more as you read on.

Sammādiṭṭhi is the Foundation of Practice

The communication and dispensation of the Buddhist religion would not be complete without a witness. Buddha thought of the two tāpasa and had *ñāṇa* (insight) to know that the two had passed away seven days before Buddha's own enlightenment. Buddha then stated that he was regretful. If only the two had the opportunity to listen to his preaching, then they would have attained emancipation in this lifetime. In the past, the two tāpasa had cultivated enough *pāramī* to achieve *arahantship*, but they practiced an incorrect method. They were stuck in the rut of tranquil meditation, infatuated with *arupajhāna* and *rupajhāna*. Once they passed away, they were reborn in *arupabrahma* where they would carry out an eternally long life there. When the Buddha Metteya arises in the world, these two will not have departed from the *brahma* existence. Despite the sufficient *pāramī* to attain *arahantship* in that lifetime, the incorrect mode of practice closed off the possibility of emancipation.

The same goes for the times in which we live. If an individual had cultivated enough *pāramī* to attain a level of emancipation, but practiced a method that strayed from that which Buddha delineated, then that person would also be closed off from the possibility of emancipation. This is because the way of practice that will bring one into the *magga* (path) of nirvana is limited. There is only one way, and it is called *sammādiṭṭhi*, correct perception aligned with the truth. If the foundation of *sammādiṭṭhi* cannot be laid down in this lifetime, the chances of finding the path to nirvana are zero. This is because in this day and age there are people who teach different methods. These masters are confident their methods of practice are correct. In this era, no one will be able to help anyone else. It will be likened to 'every man for himself.' Even if the *magga* is not found in this lifetime, the current way of practice still cultivates *pāramī* for future births.

Buddha had delivered a discourse in *Dhammacakkappavattana Sutta* (Discourse on the Wheel of Dhamma) to the five *pañcavaggiya* (the five Bhikkhus) at the Isipatana Migadāya (deer forest) in Benares. Buddha's deliverance of his very first discourse is of paramount importance. It can be said that this is where the roots of Buddhism were planted. There was the *ratanattaya* (the Triple Gem), which is the *buddharatanat, dhammaratanat* and *sangharatanat* which we know of today. Buddha used *sammādiṭṭhi* (correct perception of the truth) and *sammāsaṅkappa* (using *paññā* to contemplate according to the truth) to illustrate the first step of practice. These two are grouped under *paññā* (insight-wisdom). *Sammādiṭṭhi* itself is of the utmost importance in dhamma. Thus,

Hatthi patang taesang akkamakkayati
Sammādiṭṭhi taesang dhammanang akkamakkayati

The footprints of all legged animals are encompassed by a footprint of an elephant
Likewise, all dhamma is encompassed by *sammādiṭṭhi*

Sammādiṭṭhi, right understanding, is the starting point for practice. Correct perception of the truth is the commander leading the way to all other dhamma.

Sammāsaṅkappa is the use of *paññā* to contemplate according to the truth.

Sammāvācā is right speech, or speech that is true and fair.

Sammākammanta is right action, or action according to what is just.

Sammā-ājīva is right livelihood, or conducting a life and business that is moral and legal.

Sammāvāyāma is right effort. This means fair and just diligence in actions, speech, and thought.

Sammāsati is right mindfulness.

Sammāsamādhi is right concentration.

The seven *magga* are encompassed in *sammādiṭṭhi*, correct perception of the truth. Likened to a hen with seven chicks, whichever direction the hen takes, the chicks follow. Thus, all seven *magga* follow *sammādiṭṭhi*. *Sammādiṭṭhi* is the main artery for all dhamma. Those practitioners who have *sammādiṭṭhi* are essentially on their way to the Noble Path. Continuous practice on the Noble Path will lend to an opportunity to enter *lokuttara* (*sotapanna, sakadagami, anagami*) in this lifetime. Many people assert that if one does not practice according to four *satipaṭṭhāna* (foundations of mindfulness), then emancipation is not possible. This kind of definite statement is due to four *satipaṭṭhāna* being founded on *sammādiṭṭhi*.

Many people assert that practice must transpire in *ariyasaccāni*, the Four Noble Truths. These are *dukkha* (suffering), *samudaya* (the cause or origin of suffering), *nirodha* (cessation or extinction of suffering), and *magga* (the path leading to the cessation of suffering). Similarly, before knowing and understanding *dukkha*, before knowing and understanding the cause of *dukkha*, before reaching *nirodha* (the cessation of suffering), everything starts at the Noble Eightfold Path. And the Noble Eightfold Path begins with *sammādiṭṭhi*, correct perception of the truth. Even though there are multitudes of categories and classifications, everything takes off from *sammādiṭṭhi*. Therefore, understand this because *sammādiṭṭhi* is an important starting point that governs all other existing dhamma. Why did Buddha classify dhamma in various categories? It is because the character and *pāramī* of individuals differ, so the models and examples used for each person or group of people differs accordingly. Many people and many groups assert that if practice does not follow *abhidhamma*, then there is definitely no way that one will become an arriyapuggala. The people who assert this are under-educated and unknowledgeable. They have read one book and asserted this fixed claim.

Research the History of Arriyapuggala

Buddha delivered a discourse to Phra Yasa and his fifty five disciples. They all achieved *arahantship*. He also preached to the parents of Phra Yasa, who were the first to attain *sotapanna* in the Buddha Gotama era. After the close of the rains retreat, Buddha had them disperse and communicate the teachings to others. Buddha went to deliver a discourse to the thirty *bhattavakī* who all achieved *arahantship*. He also preached to the three *jaṭila* (matted hair ascetics, usually worshipping fire) and their one thousand followers, and all attained *arahantship*. He delivered a discourse to King Pimpisan and his court of one hundred twenty thousand. One hundred ten thousand of these people attained *sotapanna*, while the remaining ten thousand who lacked *pāramī* remained to carry on the Triple Gem and cultivate more *pāramī*.

In the first rains retreat many people listened to Buddha's discourses and attained *arahantship*. At the end of the rains retreat, these *arahants* were sent to proclaim the teachings. Each *arahant* was knowledgeable in *sammādiṭṭhi* and had examples and parallels to explain this to those who possessed *micchādiṭṭhi* (wrong or false view). These misperceptions were thus corrected so that these individuals possessed *sammādiṭṭhi*. As an example, Elder Asaji preached to Upatissa (Sāriputta) by saying,

Yaedhamma haedhu bhappawa
Taesang haetu tathāgato
Taesanjayo nirothoja
Awangwati mahasammano

Of those things that arise from a cause,
the Tathāgato has told the cause,
And also what their cessation is: This is the doctrine of the Great Recluse.

With these words, Upatissa, who had great wisdom and *sammādiṭṭhi*, achieved *arriyasotapanna*. From there Upatissa shared this short stanza with his friend, Kolita (Moggallana), who then was also established as a *sotapanna*. During the era of Buddha Gotama, he and his disciples used *sammādiṭṭhi* as the foundation for teachings. Even under other headings or categories, every subject is related to *sammādiṭṭhi*. The main purpose of these discourses is for listeners to develop the right mindset by changing incorrect perception to correct perception. Other categories of teachings followed thereafter.

I have used these individuals as examples because they are credible testimonies. What did Buddha teach in those times that so many people were able to become arriyapuggala (noble individuals)? Review the reasons that I have partially touched on. To which groups of people did he teach *sila*, the precepts? To which groups did he teach *sammādhi*, tranquil meditation, for the purpose of cultivating wisdom? Research the history of those who were arriyapuggala in those times. I have done this research, and nowhere in the texts, the eight volumes of the *Dhammapada* (Anthology of Sayings of the Buddha), or the *Sutta* (discourses, sermons, or dialogues of Buddha) does it say to meditate towards tranquility for the purpose of generating *paññā* (wisdom). So then why is this taught in present times? Study the histories of arriyapuggala and understand the foundations of the teachings Buddha demarcated. This way, one will not have qualms or question the precepts and dhamma. There will not be obstacles or doubt in upholding the precepts and dhamma. The mind will not be uncertain with regards to the precepts and one's dhamma practice will move forward and progress.

If one practices while uncertain in the precepts and dhamma, one will not be confident in oneself. Therefore, one will not be brave enough to put every effort into dhamma. First, there will be uncertainty about the precepts. Then, it will be about dhamma, constantly wondering if the practice is right or wrong. There will not be forward progress because one cannot rely on oneself nor make decisions. One will not be able to rely on *sati* (concentration), *paññā* (wisdom), or one's ability. Buddha said,

Attahi attano nattho
One is one's own refuge

Being one's own refuge relates to concentration and wisdom, and relying on one's ability and reasoning. It does not mean seeking answers from others. If others understand the way to practice, then you will be considered fortunate. If not, you will be out of luck. You will receive subjective and haphazard instruction lacking guarantees or any responsibility. Those who practice will encounter inconclusive advice and wander like a blind man trying to find his way out of a pool. In the same vein, those who practice and do not understand the correct way will wander endlessly. If one does not understand which heading of dhamma corresponds to one's character, it will be difficult to enter the *magga* (path) to nirvana. Even with sufficient *pāramī* to become an arriyapuggala in this lifetime, if one practices a method that does not correspond to what is familiar, that *pāramī* will not be of any assistance.

Dhamma practice in this era has an emphasis on *sati* (concentration) and *sammādhi* (tranquil meditation). No one is interested in practicing *sati* and *paññā* (wisdom). Perhaps it is because people do not understand and do not know how to practice in this way that this method is not taught. *Sati sampajañña*, having a clear consciousness and awareness of emotions that arise can be done, but it is not the means. Rather, it is the end result. Simply knowing or identifying emotions as they arise cannot eliminate the problems that trigger these emotions. These emotions are the result of a cause. And that cause, is wanting. If only the cause is destroyed, then the emotions will disappear as well.

As an analogy, a poisonous snake we desire to kill resides in a hole. But we are focused on staring at the hole, and when the snake pokes its head out and sees us, it retracts immediately. It is impossible to catch the snake. This is likened to using *sati sampajañña* to be aware of emotions. If *kilesas* (defilements) and *taṇhā* (greed) are to be completely destroyed, there must be *sati-paññā* that is clever and smart. This is like catching the snake. If we are completely hidden and the snake cannot see us, we can watch the snake every second that passes. Once the snake does not see us, it will slide out of the hole in its entirety. Then we will take a rock or a tree branch and cover the hole so that the snake cannot get back in there. From there, take a weapon like a sword and kill the snake. Thus, the snake will be unable to use its poisons against us ever again. As such, the models, examples and methods of those who possess *sati-paññā,* that can be used to eliminate *kilesas* and *taṇhā* from the mind, are just the same. Practicing dhamma with individual *sati-paññā,* an encompassing astute knowledge and personal ability will make it easy to extinguish *kilesas* and *taṇhā* from the mind.

Paññāya parisujjhati

The mind can be pure because of *paññā* (wisdom)

All of those who practice should understand this.

Paññāvimutti and Cetovimutti

Paññāvimutti

In this era, practitioners do not know their individual character. If one has the *paññāvimutti* character but practices the conventions of the *cetovimutti* character, then results of practice will not emerge. Likewise, those who possess *cetovimutti* character but apply the methods of *paññāvimutti* will also not see any advancement. Therefore, practitioners must figure out what type of intrinsic character they possess and practice accordingly. This way, time will not be wasted on achieving results. In the era of Buddha Gotama, most people possessed *paññāvimutti* character. Seventy percent of those who practiced and achieved emancipation were *paññāvimutti*. Research the suttas to find the accounts of arriyapuggala who had attained holiness. This includes both ascetics and lay people and the different levels of emancipation: *sotapanna*, *sakadagami, anagami,* and *arahant.* It can be immediately discerned that the majority attained holiness through *paññāvimutti.* Upon listening to a discourse, some became an arriyapuggala immediately while others used *paññā* (wisdom) to contemplate further and soon thereafter became an arriyapuggala.

One who practices must take notice of oneself during meditation to discern whether the mind desires tranquility or to focus and think. If the mind is inclined towards serenity, let it further reside in tranquility. Once the mind is released from this state, use *paññā* to contemplate issues immediately. These people are grouped in *cetovimutti.* **Those who are of *paññāvimutti* are those who like to think once the mind is focused. If you are one of these, stop meditating and instead use *paññā* to consider *saccadhamma* (truths).** It is because our character is as such that we cannot force our minds to be serene and tranquil.

Many orders teach meditation and differ in their teachings. These are quite astray from that which was practiced in the Buddha's time. In that era, meditation was done to be free of wanting and desires. In this age, meditation is done for the purpose of wanting. For example, meditation is done to fulfill the desire to possess *jhāna* (absorptions, states of mental concentration), *abhiññā*, purity of the mind, and the elimination of *kilesas* and *taṇhā*. There is a desire for *paññā* to emerge from meditation. An understanding exists that once *paññā* arises, *kilesas* and *taṇhā* will be eliminated from the mind and one will automatically become an arriyapuggala. This kind of understanding differs immensely from that which Buddha taught. Why is it taught and practiced to desire *nimitta* (visions, omens)? Once people emerge from meditation, the master will ask, "Did you see anything? What did you see?" Those who experience *nimitta* see the sky, *devas*, *niraya* (hell), or *pittivisaya* (hungry ghosts). Sometimes it is a clear, round object, other times it is something different. Those who have not experienced any *nimitta*, consequently desire to have one. So, people meditate to experience *nimitta*. In some places, states of the mind are discussed and then qualified as different levels of *jhāna*. During the times of Buddha, what disciple did he appoint to discuss and qualify these states of mind like people nowadays are doing? There are many other differing methods of meditation. In the era of Buddha, meditation was only to boost *paññā*, not for the purpose of motivating this or that to arise, like it is in current times.

Meditation, without careful research, can easily result in mistakes. Normal meditation without desires will not be problematic. But when meditation is done for the serious fulfillment of desires for this and that, it will cause the problematic ten *vipassanūpakilesas* (imperfections or defilements of insight) to arise. Meditators who lack education will have no idea that their meditation has taken a wrong turn. Instead, they will be seriously focused and determined, expecting considerable results. Thus *micchādiṭṭhi* (wrong or false view) arises. A false perception that is not corrected is *micchādiṭṭhi*. Determination that is wrong turns into the ten *vipassanūpakilesas*. I have explained this in detail in my book, "Paradigm Shift." You can find it, read it, and you will fully and clearly understand this issue.

Cetovimutti

Those who have the *cetovimutti* character have previously been born as *isi* (sage, seer) or *tāpasa* (ascetic). They have practiced *sammādhi* (meditation), *jhāna* (absorptions, states of mental concentration), and *abhiññā* (supernormal, higher psychic powers) until these were ingrained in their character. However, these people never practiced *sati-paññā* (consciousness-wisdom) in contemplating *saccadhamma* (truth) in any way. There was only steadfast determination in *sammādhi, jhāna,* and *abhiññā*. Once these people were reborn in contemporary times, their practice was consequently the same as that of past births, as they were content with tranquil meditation, *jhāna*, and *abhiññā*. As *jhāna* and *abhiññā* arise, they will reach a dead end, practicing in endless circles of tranquil meditation, *jhāna*, and *abhiññā*. They will not know of the way out that leads to the emancipation from the world. They will be infatuated and attached to these methods until the day they die.

People with *cetovimutti* character cannot be taught how to use *sati-paññā* (consciousness-wisdom) in contemplating *saccadhamma* (truth) in one fell swoop. Buddha knew exactly how to instruct these types of individuals. He had to teach them to enter tranquil meditation and *jhāna* until there was no way out. At the dead end, there would be circular progress and they would have to start with *jhāna* all over again. This is likened to the analogy of the blind man trying to find his way out of a pool.

At this point, Buddha will force them to turn over a new leaf. He will critique and provide them with suggestions as to motivate the realization that the serenity from tranquil meditation and *jhāna* is only temporary. This is the method that Bhikkhu Siddhāttha had walked through, himself. And it is neither the way to become an arriyapuggala (a noble person) nor the *magga* (path) to nirvana. Upon death, these people will be reborn in the *brahma* realm and live extensively long lives. At the end of a *brahma* life, these people will be reborn in the human world once again. They will be lost and astray, without any goal or target. These people will follow the norms in place in the world in an endless cycle.

Buddha provided instructions as follows. Once serenity is reached in tranquil meditation, maintain that state. Soon after, there will be a release from that tranquility. Right as the mind is releasing from that state, be focused, conscious, and control the release from the tranquility such that it is incomplete[2]. The part that is still serene to

---

[2] This is similar to waking up in the morning. Before fully awakening, do not open your eyes. Use this

an extent is called *sammādhi* (meditation) which is focused and determined, and is also known as *upacara sammādhi*. Use *paññā* (insight-wisdom) to contemplate the previous *dosa* (destructive consequences) and *bhaya* (peril) inherent in attaining *jhāna*, such that one realizes that it is not the way to eliminate *kilesas* (defilements, desires) or *taṇhā* (greed) from the mind. **Practicing serenity in meditation and being attached to and infatuated with *jhāna* is likened to a stone sitting atop blades of grass.** Once the stone is picked up, the blades of grass will stand up and grow just as before. **The mind that is infatuated with and attached to the tranquility from meditation and *jhāna* merely sits on top of *kilesas* and *taṇhā*.** Once serenity in meditation

---

partially awake and fully conscious state to contemplate your dream or any other issues. Your consciousness will be especially sharp and keen. In meditation, the incomplete release from the tranquil state (*upacara sammādhi*) is likened to the partially awake and fully conscious state described here.

and *jhāna* dissolve, *kilesas* and *taṇhā*, both small and large, will stand up and grow in the mind just as before.

Those people will then use *paññā* (insight-wisdom) to realize and understand the realities of *saccadhamma* (the ultimate truth), the four elements (earth, air, fire, water) and five *khanda* (the aggregates: *rupa*-perceived form, *vedanā*-feeling, *saññā*-memory, *saṅkhāra*-mental formations, and *viññāna*-consciousness) according to the Three Common Characteristics. That is, *annicca* (impermanence), *dukkha* (suffering), and *anattā* (cessation of existence in the supposed form). Contemplate such that there is realization and understanding of the human body as filthy and repulsive. Soon thereafter, the body will fall and decompose back into the four elements of this earth, just as before. With repeated and constant contemplation of these matters, those people will experience *nibbidā* (dispassion, disinterest) and boredom with pleasure, passion, and lust. The mind will then escape into nirvana. Therefore, the *arahants* of this nature are deemed *cetovimutti*. ***Cetovimutti* is those who have previously practiced serene meditation and *jhāna* and have come to use *paññā* to contemplate *saccadhamma* afterwards.** Once attaining *arahantship*, recreational use of *jhāna* and *abhiññā* is not problematic.

Discernment to Contemplate the Three Common Characteristics

The mind's infatuation with the world is called *avijjā* (ignorance, delusion), which is ignorance of *saccadhamma* (the truth) that has permitted the infatuation with *kilesas* (defilements, desires) and *saṅkhāra* (volitional mental formations). Whichever direction *kilesas* and *taṇhā* (greed) desire to take, *saṅkhāra* will follow. Each day, there will be volitional mental formations according to the *sammuti* (supposed forms, conventional truths) of the world. The mind is thus infatuated with the world and has since been constantly reborn in it. This is due to the misperception, misunderstanding, and infatuation of this as the correct approach. But, now that we know the truth, let us start over again. **Practice thinking in the way of *annicca*, that everything is impermanent, subject to change, and never to**

perpetually maintain its state. Think in terms of the suffering that we experience as a repercussion from a particular cause. What is that cause? Once the cause of suffering is discerned, then stop that cause. Even if desires and wanting arise, restrain the mind so that it is patient. Practice so that the mind has these characteristics, so the mind will be manageable and less frustrated.

Practice such that the mind knows how to refuse. Constantly train the mind to understand that within this world, nothing is a personal belonging. Money, gold, and possessions are merely worldly belongings that exist in this world. No matter how little or how much, understand that they are only factors that enable day to day survival. In a few days, whether sooner or later, there will be a departure from these worldly belongings. If one is still worried and clinging to these worldly possessions, one will keep being reborn in the world. Without end, whatever the mind clings to, it will be reborn with. This is just like what has occurred from past lives to the present. Because of clinging to worldly possessions, we have been reborn again and again and will consequently die in the same fashion as before. Are you ready to refuse worldly belongings at this time? Constantly employ *sati* (consciousness) and *paññā* (wisdom) to train the mind to refuse these things. The mind will gradually loosen its attachment. Money and riches should be considered communal belongings within the family. Do not cling to these possessions such that suffering arises.

Suffering arises when we perceive an object as a personal belonging. The degree of suffering is directly correlated with the level of attachment to these belongings. If attachment is not present, then suffering of the mind does not arise as a result. It is not that acquiring these possessions is prohibited, because we still have a need to sustain our physical human form. It is necessary to earn a living and find food to enable our earthly forms to survive. Cultivate *pāramī* in

and decay and will be cremated in a fire. Only ashes will remain. There will be no way to construct a human from those ashes. This is *anattā*. Use *paññā* (wisdom) to contemplate this regularly.

The mind will realize according to the truth once *paññā* (wisdom) is used for this contemplation. This realization is called *sammādiṭṭhi*, which is correct and just perception, along with an understanding of the truth. *Sammādiṭṭhi* is classified as either *tassanañāṇa* (realization followed by understanding corresponding to the truth) or *ñāṇatassana* (understanding followed by realization corresponding to the truth).

Resources for Dhamma Practice

There are two methods of practice:

1. Training by prohibiting thought. This is a method of continually focusing on any one phrase, or consciously concentrating on the emotions that emerge from the mind. This is the mode of prohibiting thought.

2. Training by using thought to analyze *saccadhamma*. For example, upon seeing an elderly and sick person, internalize that image and use personal reflection to see that another person's aging and sickness is the same as that which will occur to us. Let that parallel attribute the same characteristics to that person as well as us. We too will age, become sick, and pass away just like everyone else because everyone is born from elements that age, become sick, and pass away. Once born, life will persist for a period and then death will take over. The understanding of these common characteristics is *sammādiṭṭhi*, which is

correct and just understanding of the truth. Upon understanding this concept, the first level of *paññā* (wisdom) has been initiated. *Paññā*, realization, and understanding of other *saccadhamma* will expand. The realization and understanding of the mind will be more lucid and obvious. This is deemed, *yonisomanasikāra* (proper consideration, having thorough method in one's thought). Detailed and thorough understanding of issues that were previously confusing will suddenly emerge.

Cittam dantam sukhāvaham

The mind that is well trained in wisdom will have encompassing and lucid knowledge of *saccadhamma*, and the mind will be peaceful at all times.

Doubt or contempt for the truth will not exist because the all-encompassing *paññā* (wisdom) will have eliminated all doubt from the mind. Where will the clinging and attachment come from? Thus, using *paññā* to train the mind is incredibly important, just as it is important for parents to teach their children to be good. *Paññā* used to train the mind to develop wide and encompassing knowledge is the same. Normally, the mind believes its wrong perceptions are right and that is why the mind is ignorant and delusional. This nescience called *avijjā* (absence of knowledge), the mind's blindness and existence in the dark.

A blind mind refers to a mind without *paññā* (wisdom), just like a person who is congenitally blind. Tasks cannot be successfully completed that involve travelling to a completely foreign location. This task is excruciatingly difficult for the blind. Likewise, a blind mind that lacks wisdom to realize *saccadhamma* does not know the methods or examples to use in practice. Arriving at the *magga* (path) and results is excruciatingly difficult. These days, the Buddha is not present to identify the parallels and examples to use in order arrive at the *magga* to nirvana.

Thus, practitioners must rely on their own consciousness, wisdom, and ability.

If incorrect knowledge is drawn from *pariyatti* (the Scriptures), then incorrect perception called *micchādiṭṭhi* will result. If these conclusions are applied in practice, then *micchā* (wrong) practice will result.

In his time, Buddha used examples to teach everyone how to eliminate *micchādiṭṭhi*, as the first step. People who practice in our times only understand the *pariyatti* version of *sammādiṭṭhi*. This is why they are not able to extinguish the deep misunderstandings they possess in their minds. Misperception, misunderstanding, and delusion are characteristics that have been long ingrained within the mind. This ignorance is thus called *avijjā*, the mind's blindness. The mind is ignorant of its misunderstandings and, because it is unaware, misinterprets its perceptions as right. Knowledge carried from Scriptures is nothing more than knowledge. It cannot be used to untangle or ameliorate misunderstandings.

Therefore, concentration and wisdom must be practiced so that an intelligent and encompassing knowledge emerges within one's mind. Call on this knowledge for analysis and examination until discernment of right and wrong emerges. Make decisions on the basis of fair and just reason. If decisions are biased and self-interested, the misunderstanding of misperceptions as correct will continue to occur. Understand what is right according to the truth. Once people have established the foundation of correct understanding, practicing dhamma will be easy because they would have entered the *magga* (path) to nirvana. Those people will be confident that their way of practice is exactly the same as what Buddha had intended.

Interpret Buddha's Teachings Well

In current times, many masters and sects claim to practice Buddha's way. Upon observation, these methods are incongruent, while each asserts that its practice is correct. As a consequence, different sects have emerged. This is like blind men groping an elephant. Wherever one man touches, he believes that part corresponds to the whole elephant. Each man believes he truly understands what the elephant is. In the same vein, in our times each sect believes it truly understand the Buddha's history. Problems arise from discrepancies in perception. So factions have arisen, as we know:

1. Mahāyāna
2. Therāvada

Within these two schools, there are differing views on Buddha's teachings. As a result, there are even more divisions within these factions.

Interpretation of Buddha's teachings after the fifth *saṅgīti* (a council of the Sangha in order to settle questions of doctrine and to fix the text of the Scriptures) had passed. Then there was the era of *attakhataccan*, knowledgeable scholars who inherited and maintained the religion. In this period, interpretations, changes and additions were made to Buddha's teachings. While many of Buddha's teachings are reliable, others have been rearranged so that the order does not directly correspond to the original teachings. To illustrate, the three *sikkhā* (training, discipline) as people know it is *sīla*, *sammādhi,* and *paññā* (precepts, meditation and wisdom, respectively) have been abridged from the Noble Eightfold Path.

Instead of keeping the original order that Buddha laid down, it has been rearranged:

Sammādiṭṭhi and *sammāsaṅkappa* both fall under the *paññā* heading.

Sammāvācā, *sammākammanta* and *sammā-ājīva* all fall under the *sīla* heading.

Sammāvāyāma, *sammāsati* and *sammāsamādhi* all fall under the *sammādhi* heading.

The three *sikkhā* according to the original grouping is *paññā*, *sīla*, and then *sammādhi*. In Buddha's era, many of the followers he taught were able to become arriyapuggala (noble persons). This is because the path Buddha had delineated was the correct and true starting point. In our era, *sīla, sammādhi, paññā* is practiced. Research for the sake of knowledge is fine. But if that knowledge is to be applied to practice, it is crucial to use Buddha's original teaching of *paññā, sīla, sammādhi*.

The reason I have expressed this opinion is because there is reliable evidence. Thus the Pali phrase Buddha proclaimed,

Asa dhammo sanantano

All dhamma is ancient

Many meanings can be derived from the phrase, "all dhamma is ancient." I will explain it in terms of the Noble Eightfold Path, which itself is ancient. The Noble Eightfold Path is a heading that can be used in both *lokiya* (worldly) and *lokuttara* (transcendental) dhamma practice. It depends on which character with which the practitioner is more comfortable. All the previous Buddhas have started their teachings with the Noble Eightfold Path, especially *sammādiṭṭhi* (correct perception of the truth) and *sammāsaṅkappa* (*paññā* to contemplate according to the truth). These are ancient truths. The methods of practice all pointed in the same direction. Thus,

Sabba-pāpassa akaranam kusalassūpa sampada
Sacitta-pariyodapanam etam buddhāna-sāsanam

These three headings are the teachings of every Buddha. It is evidently clear that these three subjects are contained in the Noble Eightfold Path. The translation is: abstinence from committing bad deeds of action, speech and thought; the perpetuation of committing good deeds of action, speech and thought; the constant practice of mind purification; these are the teachings of all Buddhas, which is ancient. Understand this accordingly.

***Sammādiṭṭhi*, in particular, is the center of all dhamma headings or subjects.** All Buddhas must start from *sammādiṭṭhi*, correct perception. The realization and understanding of the truth all transpire in the same manner. *Āsavakkhayañāṇa* and the realization that *āsava* (mental intoxications, defilements) will cease arises and occurs in the same fashion. The enlightenment of every Buddha is the same. *Kilesas* (defilements, desires), *taṇhā* (greed), and *āsava*, both small and large, are completely extinguished in the same way. You all know that

Buddha was enlightened by the Four Noble Truths. *Dukkha, samudaya, magga,* and *nirodha* are all ancient truths and all Buddhas must be enlightened in the same way. This is the tradition of all Buddhas.

All of the disciples of Buddha Kakusanto, Buddha Konagamana, Buddha Kassapa, and Buddha Gotama had *āsavakkhayañāṇa* and the realization that *āsava* will cease occur the same way. Achieving *arahantship* was consequently the same. Even the disciples of Buddha Metteya and other Buddhas to come, will all have *āsavakkhayañāṇa* (knowledge that *āsava* will cease) in the same manner. Therefore, dhamma that is ancient has been around forever. And arriyapuggala (noble persons) of other levels reached emancipation by ancient dhamma, as well.

There is another ancient dhamma that Buddha has stated,

Hatthi patang taesang akkamakkayati
Sammādiṭṭhi taesang dhammanang akkamakkayati

> **The footprints of all legged animals are encompassed by a footprint of an elephant**
> **Likewise, all dhamma is encompassed by *sammādiṭṭhi***

If one understands the meaning of Buddha's statement, one will immediately understand that *sammādiṭṭhi* is the starting point for all dhamma. Whether it is under *paññā, sīla, sammādhi,* or any other heading, everything is encompassed by *sammādiṭṭhi*. Dhamma practice must start correctly, according to Buddha's teachings, in order to be fruitful. Consider that training nowadays is confusing and messed up because the starting point is incorrect. And educated scholars interpret and define Buddha's teachings in a perplexing manner. Researchers understand according to the Scriptures, but if the

Scriptures are incorrect and the interpretation is incorrect, then the resulting understanding is also incorrect.

People who practice the Four Noble Truths these days differ in understanding and consequently, in practice. If someone possesses wisdom and draws the correct meaning from the Four Noble Truths, then that person will have an opportunity to become an arriyapuggala in this lifetime.

A person may become an arriyapuggala in this lifetime for three reasons:

1. *Pubbekatapuññatā*: the state of having done meritorious actions in the past

2. *Sammādiṭṭhi*: the correct understanding of the truth as Buddha has laid forth.

3. *Sammāvāyāma*: continuous diligence, during every *iriyāpatha* (four postures).

If someone has satisfied these three conditions, then that person will attain some level of arriyapuggala in this lifetime. In current times, practitioners must rely heavily on their *sati*, *sammādhi*, and *paññā*. The mind must train its personal ability so that it is exceptionally capable. If those who practice possess decisive ability, they will have great motivation to practice. Without ability in *sati-paññā*, training is futile. Regardless of the knowledge of various categories of dhamma, none of that knowledge can be applied to practice due to lack of ability. The headings of *sīla* and *sammādhi* are merely knowledge in literature. It is just like raw produce and animal's meat from the market. They must be crafted into the desired food product in order to be edible. Similarly, with regards to practice, selecting the strategy and dhamma heading that best corresponds to one's character will fashion a simpler path to nirvana.

Selecting the Proper Leader

Dhamma practitioners who are in search of a leader must be observant and rational. Do not conduct yourself as someone so attached to a leader that you lose sight of dhamma. This is just like a group of oxen that search for their leader to bring them across the stream. As there are many leaders of the oxen, which one will be chosen as the leader? The group of oxen must consider this and make an independent decision. Just don't select a blind ox as the leader or he might rush the group of oxen to get stuck in the stream. Instead, if the ox has good vision and knows how to get across the stream, then he will be ready to guide all the other oxen across the stream safely. This includes all oxen except those who like to go astray from the leader.

Likewise, we who are training and preparing ourselves at this time must all seek out a proper leader to guide us in the right direction. But for the leader to be proper and accurate like in Buddha's time is incredibly unlikely. In those days, Buddha was the leader and the disciples had *paṭisambhidāñāṇa* (analytic insight) and were ready to comprehensively explain things to all the followers. Furthermore, the examples of practice were all in the same format. That is why so many in that era became arriyapuggala.

Abhidhamma

The subject of *abhidhamma* (the Higher Doctrine) that we all recognize is known from the *Tipiṭaka* (Pali Canon): *Sutta* (discourses), *Vinaya* (the code of monastic discipline), and *Paramattha* (the absolute truth, *abhidhamma*). I will provide the reason that *abhidhamma* happened after Buddha was enlightened. In the fifth rains retreat, Buddha taught the doctrine to his mother in the *Tāvatiṁsa* heaven. He spent one rains retreat there, preaching *abhidhamma* to his mother and the *devas*. The details are written in texts. At the end of the rains retreat, Buddha returned to the human world and taught *abhidhamma* to Sāriputta at the town of Sangasanakorn. He did this so Sāriputta would be his witness of these teachings and so that Buddhist followers would not wonder where he was and what he was doing for three months in Tāvatiṁsa Heaven. What was the nature of *abhidhamma*? Buddha had taught Sāriputta all of it. This is the reason for *abhidhamma*. Sāriputta, who was the best in terms of wisdom, was able to remember all of the *abhidhamma* and also recorded it.

Abhidhamma is one subject out of many. It is specific and particular to selected occasions, and Buddha preached it only to the *devas*. It is too detailed for humans to comprehend. Just how detailed, you should research for your own knowledge. The *deva* realm is comprised of four *khandas* (aggregates): *vedanā* (feeling), *saññā* (memory), *saṅkhāra* (mental formations), and *viññāna* (consciousness). *Abhidhamma* has *cetesika* (mental factors and states) as its foundation, with details available in various texts. One should research the reason why *abhidhamma* came about.

Abhidhamma occurred once Buddha reached the fifth rains retreat. As for the question of what Buddha preached between the first and fourth rains retreats, the answer is that *abhidhamma* had not yet happened. So what dhamma did he preach? The texts clearly show that it was definitely not *abhidhamma.*

In Buddha's time, he preached many subjects to many followers, who attained emancipation as arriyapuggala. There is nothing in historical records stating that Buddha used *abhidhamma* to teach anyone. What is more, there is no history asserting that any person listened to *abhidhamma* from Buddha, consequently attained emancipation, and became an arriyapuggala. Sāriputta carried on the account of *abhidhamma* from Buddha for the purpose of recording it and for other monks to study. Sāriputta did not use *abhidhamma* to teach anyone else to train in that way. He knew from his own experience that when he was a lay person who listened to dhamma from Asaji, he was able to understand and attain *sotapanna.* The dhamma Asaji shared with him was not *abhidhamma*, rather it was *saccadhamma* (the truth) that everything arises from a cause and ceases when the cause ceases. If only one studies the history of arriyapuggala (noble individuals) in

Buddha's times, which is abundant in the discourses, it will be evident that Buddha used people as examples. He would illustrate that one group used one heading of dhamma to become arriyapuggala. One should study this carefully because there is ample reason to support this. And one will realize the origin of *abhidhamma* as I have previously detailed.

Conclusion

This history of the Buddha which is explained here may have many points of contention for people if they have only studied the Thai version. If the history from other countries is incorporated or combined it may be perceived that the information in incorrect. The reason is that Buddha's history is different in each country. However, the histories share similarities in some points. Therefore, the reader should use balance in weighing the reasons according to the truth. What is possible and what is not? What has sufficient reason for one to be more believable than another? As an illustration, Buddha's encountering the four divine messengers is different from the Thai version, as I have already explained.

Another point is the floating of the golden tray. There are two implications of Bhikkhu Siddhāttha's aspiration. If he would become a Buddha, the golden tray would float upstream, against the current. If he would not become a Buddha, the golden tray would follow the current as it floated downstream. The golden tray floated upstream, so Buddha used the tray as a parallel for contemplation. He internalized the parallel and compared the golden tray to his own mind. He reasoned with *paññā* and taught his own mind to float against the current of the world. He did this until wisdom emerged and he understood and realized according to the truth that everything is subject to change. There is nothing that maintains perpetually. But humans cannot accept this impermanence, and thus experience suffering. Humans do not desire to be apart from belongings, and consequently both the clinging and the perception that we are defined by those possessions arise. And the mind desires to gain, to possess, and to be. It clings tightly and is reborn in this endless cycle. Buddha had the wisdom to deny his mind from having incorrect perceptions (*micchādiṭṭhi*), incorrect understandings, and from the worldly delusions of previous lives. The

Buddha knew the cause and factors involved in birth. *Taṇhā* (greed), pleasure, attachment, and clinging tight to fine sense pleasures cause an endless rebirth in the Three Realms (*kāmaloka*: the world of sense desire, *rūpaloka*: form-sense sphere, and *arūpaloka*: formless, immaterial sphere). Buddha used wisdom to contemplate this extensively. *Ñāṇatassana* arose in Buddha's mind and he understood and realized the truth. *Vipassanañāṇa* and *āsavakkhayañāṇa* emerged and he was enlightened as a Buddha because of this.

There is another point concerning *ñāṇatassana*, which means understanding before realization. For example, understanding from someone's description that a tiger looks like this or that, without actually seeing one. This is a trait of *ñāṇatassana*, understanding without seeing or realizing. *Tassanañāṇa* relates to realization before understanding. For instance, upon seeing a tiger in real life but not understanding what it is, one might venture to guess that it is a big cat. This is likened to the fisherman that was explained earlier. Understanding on its own is not sufficient. Therefore, understanding without realization may result in a mistake. Realization on its own may produce similar results.

In the texts, only *ñāṇatassana* is described. *Tassanañāṇa* was encountered in the Laotian versions, which contained reason and credibility. That is why I have written about it here for you to study. True understanding indicates *ñāṇa*, while true realization relates to *tassana* (wisdom). Dhamma practice must incorporate both understanding as well as realization so that results materialize. This is just like how clapping with two hands produces sound, while clapping with one hand does not. Training in present times does mention *ñāṇatassana* to a small degree because it is touched on in texts.

In practice, there is only a *ñāṇa* that understands emotions have arisen, but there is no realization of the cause behind those emotions. Or in the alternate case, one speaks from manuals without personal understanding. The mind will never loosen its clinging and attachment to various objects. This is like seeing the image of a tiger on paper and understanding that it is a tiger. There is no fear. But once a tiger is seen in real life, fear will arise. Understanding from manuals without realizing the truth is likened to only understanding dhamma by name, without realizing dhamma. Similarly, this is like knowing the name of a criminal without ever seeing his face. It is impossible to catch the criminal. In the same vein, learning dhamma from manuals will not eliminate *kilesas, taṇhā,* or misperceptions within the mind. Or sometimes people understand *saccadhamma* (the truth) but see it as a normal and common occurrence, like seeing an old person, a sick person, and a deceased person. These people are not smart. They do not have the insight to know that the truth of what they have seen are the suffering, *dosa* (destructive consequences), and *bhaya* (perils) that cause countless rebirths in this endless cycle.

I apologize for the example that follows. If one takes a photograph of fresh feces, the photograph will not incite disgust. It is possible to eat dinner while looking the photograph without being repulsed. If you are brave enough, bring the fresh feces to the dinner table while you are eating. Once you see and smell it at the same time, what do you feel? Likewise, practicing dhamma with both *ñāṇatassana* (understanding and realization) and *tassanañāṇa* (realization and understanding), according to *saccadhamma*, will correct false perceptions from *micchādiṭṭhi* to *sammādiṭṭhi*.

Buddha used wisdom to contemplate the truth and his mind achieved *sammādiṭṭhi* (correct and just perception) and *sammāsaṅkappa* (*paññā* to contemplate according to the truth). Buddha thus announced and guaranteed that he had encountered the correct path to enlightenment on his own. This is because *saccadhamma* is the ancient truth which has been around forever. Humans do not recognize this *saccadhamma* and are consequently delusional because they lack wisdom to understand and realize these worldly truths. Buddha used *sammādiṭṭhi* as the initial starting point and the central foundation for other subjects.

Upon reading this book, you may encounter many parts that cause you to wonder. If you have any questions, please ask me directly. If you ask someone else, their perception and interpretation may be different. If you have any quandaries from the texts and manuals you have read, I am ready to be your council so that you can develop understanding from foundations of reason, cause, and effect. Use the truth as the deciding factor. If you have any misgivings from the books I have written, or from any subject of dhamma, ask me directly. If you have tied a knot and cannot undo it, I will do it for you.

With the power of sati, *sammādhi*, *paññā*, and *pāramī* cultivated from past lives, may you understand and realize the truth, *saccadhamma*, with your own *sati* and *paññā*.

Venerable Ācariya Thoon Khippapanyo

About the Author

Venerable Ācariya Thoon Khippapanyo (Phra Banyāpisantaera) was born in 1935, and or dained as a monk in 1961. He was a pupil of renowned Venerable Ācariya Khao Analayo of Wat Tam Klong Paen in the Nong Bua Lam Phu province of Thailand. In his early years, Ācariya Thoon set out to various forest destinations and practiced dhamma until he profoundly realized and understood according to the truth that Buddha had laid forth.

In 1985 Ācariya Thoon built and established Wat Pa Ban Koh in Udon Thani as a site for dedicated practitioners to train in Buddha's dhamma. In 2001, a majestic pagoda was erected from the immense faith of Ācariya Thoon's numerous devoted followers both in Thailand and overseas.

He has authored over twenty highly acclaimed books on dhamma practice, both in Thai and translated into English. Ācariya Thoon teaches an approach to dhamma that emphasizes the cultivation of individual sati, *sammādhi*, and *paññā* (mindfulness, alert and focused concentration, and insight-wisdom) and their application in the solving of personal problems. He has successfully developed a unique and practical method for lay people to eliminate the suffering that emerges in their daily lives.

About the Translator

San Francisco native Neecha Thian-Ngern holds a Bachelors of Science in Electrical Engineering from UC San Diego and a Masters in Business Administration. Neecha has been a devout follower of Venerable Ācariya Thoon since the age of 16.

For many years, Neecha's mother Saranya was on an unfruitful quest to encounter a master to illuminate the path to cessation of suffering. Skeptical by nature, Neecha never felt moved by any inconclusive sermons or shaky logic inherent in many dhamma discussions. Through a single, brief, and pivotal encounter with Ācariya Thoon, she was able to see that she must first circumvent and catch the snake instead of focusing on the person who threw it at her. Neecha also came to realize the most crucial and undisputable truth-that she was the sole cause for all of her stress and suffering. From that point on, armed with Ācariya Thoon's concentrated and insightful models of dhamma practice, she applied simple parallels from her daily surroundings to scrub away at her personal anguish and attachments. She extracted and confronted her feelings, and worked to realize and understand the truth behind them. Through the constant application of rational internalized reflection, Neecha has been able to dramatically limit the frequency of her emotional volcanic eruptions as well as conflicts with friends and family. Deeply grateful for Ācariya Thoon's unique and viable approach to dhamma practice, she is inspired to communicate his message to the English speaking public.